CORPORATE DECEPTIONS

About the Author

The author is a serving police officer in Kerala. He secured his post-graduation in economics from S.N. College, Kannur. Before joining police service he had taught economics to post graduate students for a brief stint of 4 years. He is a renowned investigating officer in Kerala police and had rich experience of probing high profile crimes over varied subjects including economic scams, terrorism, homicides and organized crimes, over a period of more than two decades. This book is the result of his extensive research into the modus operandi of MLM Companies and is part of his investigative encounter with some corporate firms which had siphoned off thousands of crores of rupees from the poor investors.

Author is married to Sreeja and is blessed with two children, Daya and Dhyan.

CORPORATE DECEPTIONS

P.P. Sadanandan Chengalayi

CONCEPT PUBLISHING COMPANY PVT. LTD.
NEW DELHI-110059

ISBN-13: 978-93-5125-294-8

First Published 2017

Published and Printed by

Concept
Since 1974

Concept Publishing Company Pvt. Ltd.
Regd. Office:
A/15-16, Commercial Block, Mohan Garden,
New Delhi-110059 (INDIA)
Phones : 25351460, 25351794, *Fax* : 091-11-25357109
Email : publishing@conceptpub.com
Website: www.conceptpub.com

Editorial Office: H-13, Bali Nagar, New Delhi-110 015, India.

Cataloging in Publication Data—DK Courtesy: D.K. Agencies (P) Ltd. <docinfo@dkagencies.com>

Sadanandan Chengalayi, P. P., author.
Corporate deceptions / P.P. Sadanandan Chengalayi.
pages cm
Includes bibliographical references and index.
ISBN 9789351252948

1. Commercial crimes—India. 2. Corporations—Corrupt practices—India. 3. Corporation law—India. I. Title.

HV6771.I4S23 2017 DDC 364.1680954 23

Preface

The idea of the book dawned upon me during the investigation of a number of cases related to economic offences. There was a sudden spurt of cases in Kerala in which unimaginable amount of money was siphoned off from the public who invested their hard-earned income in fancy schemes.

In the initial stages of the probe itself, I became aware of the grey areas in the law that allowed these firms to take deep root in our society. As the investigation progressed, I was shocked to realize that the awareness about the treachery was abysmally poor even among the law enforcing agencies. The companies had succeeded in confusing the public and the state alike.

This prompted me to take a deep and dispassionate look at the issue involved; its ramifications in society and the threat these firms pose to our economy.

I set to sail from here at a time; there were no authentic documents to help those who wish to pursue the topic in a broader way. The news reports in the media are skin-deep, *ad-hocist* and reflect only a tip of the iceberg. The books I referred in the topic were basically subjective postulations of those who burned their fingers. Though, it offers a compelling reading with the narrations about their own experience of working in various companies, they lacked methodological rigour. They deal with the subjects in a general way, and are silent on the intricate models developed by various MLM companies.

As I delved deep, I got entangled more in the topic. Considering my keenness in the issue, my superior officers entrusted me the task of developing a professional team of investigators who are equipped to take on the companies.

I was fortunate enough to hold classes extensively for police officers on various aspects of money circulation schemes at Kerala

Police Academy and Police Training College, under the auspices of Bureau of Police Research and Development, New Delhi. It was felt in these discourses that there is need to have comprehensive analysis of the *modus operandi* of the companies running money circulation schemes.

Soon I realized that it has academic value too. I had a brief stint in the academic field also as a teacher handling post-graduate courses in Economics. During this period I was dealing with economic theories.

Strange experiences are faced by the investigating officers with even the victims of the crime turning against them, believing that the authorities are spoiling their chances of making easy money. Warning notices from the government against investing in pyramid schemes were viewed by the public as government interference to otherwise legitimate investments. The mass of investors see the chief of companies as a Folk Hero and their Savior and not as a swindler. There are instances of the investors going on hunger strike demanding the release of arrested frauds. Even there are instances of the Ministers terming the arrest and search as vulgar abuse of power. This book endeavours to recapture the storms of protests and violent outbursts of rioting against the enforcement agency following the misunderstanding and confusion created by the con men.

The study is a multipronged one. Even when analyzing the nitty-gritty of the various forms of money circulation schemes, I tried to unravel the basic models that are lying deep in all the schemes operated by the networking companies. The study relied on the facts revealed in the crime investigation, which is accurate and authentic than any other empirical research. The money circulation schemes offered by various companies are deducted into economic models and are elucidated on the basis of settled notions of economic theorems and mathematical tools.

There is a keen interest among the general public about the money circulation schemes after the police started registering cases against the companies. Every other day media is coming up with stories on these companies. They are not going to vanish from our society even in the face of strict legislation or enforcement. The students of business management and economics are being taught that network marketing is a sunrise sector with immense possibilities wide open. These pet theories and exaggerated stories are debunked here. I present a different perspective and demarcate the line between direct selling and illegal networking. Thus, I hope that the book will be enthusiastically greeted by the community of investigating officers, members of the judiciary, legislators, academicians, students and economic regulators.

I would like to express my deep felt gratitude to my friend MP Prasanth, Special Correspondent of *Times of India,* Calicut, who had done the most painstaking examination of my first draft for fine tuning the language. I must record gratitude to ADGP Sri Vinson M. Paul, in Kerala Police, for developing a new methodology for the investigation of economic offence and for endorsing me to investigate as well as to educate the investigators, which prompted me to make a deep going study in the subject.

P.P. Sadanandan Chengalayi
Kannur, Kerala

Contents

1
The Deceptive Games of Con Artistes

"Man's quest to make quick and easy money—to live not by the sweat of his brow—has been the cause of his fall from the halo of virtue on this planet".[1] The cravings to make fast and easy money by unfair ways have been the fundamental cause of injustice and criminality in all societies at all times and exposing such crimes is inevitable for the survival of all societies.

In the great work *Divine Comedy*, Dante ranked cheating as the most displeasing act to the God than any other sins like violence as it involves malicious use of reason. Depicting cheating as the most heinous of all the crimes, he placed the cheaters in the ninth circle in the inferno below all other criminals.

In modern time, tricky con men developed cheating as an art and millions of hapless victims find it difficult to take on the cheaters, who appear with diverse schemes.

Value System in Business in Times of Globalization

Exploiting the ignorance of the general public and taking advantage of the loopholes in the law, the con artistes stockpile crores of rupees, piggy riding on the confusion created by them. The so called multi-level marketing, whose tentacles are spread to even the remote villages the worldover, through an occult system of enrolling endless chain of sellers, thrives by propagating the new value system, unleashed by the fraudsters that failure to make money is a sin and lack of skill. When these dreamers realize the ultimate truth that pursuing a continuing stream of sales is only a mirage, the system teaches them to console that their financial losses are due to their own shortfalls.

It relies on a system of marketing which commercializes family and friendship, uses cult mind control techniques in the world of business and breed endless infatuations for gain carnivalizing greed and craze.

"Broad mass of people fall victim to a big lie more easily than a small one".[2] Adolf Hitler's social psychology maxim was applied to the field of business promotion by the fraudulent multinational and domestic business conglomerates who repeat lies as a tool for looting the people.

Fraudsters present their deceptive schemes as a sugar coated pill, promising fabulous return when new members are enrolled into the schemes. While the credulous get entangled into this vicious circle, the promoters market the schemes as lucrative business opportunity. They have no qualm in capitalizing on friendship and social relations to woo more and more members into the cobweb of incomprehensible schemes.

Arthur Miller's '*Death of Salesman*'[3] is the tragedy of a failed merchant who became a misfit in the business rat race, which celebrates only bandwagon of the victors and which is insensitive to the cries of the vanquished. The *modus operandi* of the con men is to trumpet the success stories of a negligible minority while keeping a tactical silence on the millions who perished chasing the mirage.

Emerging Economic Crimes

Emergence of new generation organized economic crimes that crosses the territorial boarder is the dark side of globalization. The proceeds of crime involved in the economic offences like, money circulation scheme, market manipulations, instant lotteries, plastic money scams and internet based cheating are beyond the imagination and can be expressed only as a percentage of GDP of the nations.

Internet is crammed with thousands of websites hosted by high tech fraudsters that lure the gullible public with their nefarious designs of deceptive investment schemes offering fabulous returns.

Viral proliferation of collective investment schemes, through which fund worth thousands of crores of rupees is swindled is augmented by the absence of social stigma towards economic offence and dearth of popular and political support for regulatory actions.

Globalization era is marked by the entry of dubious international firms which drained away funds from domestic economy to foreign destinations through money circulation schemes under the guise of "marketing pills, potions and lotions"[4]. Despite criminal charges and prosecution faced in several countries, with the victims numbering millions spread across the world, these companies go on recruiting endless chain of "distributors", who are deceived into working hard in pursuit of a cruel illusion.

Thousands of companies are thriving, worldover, running ponzi and pyramid schemes in so many camouflaged forms in the name of Multi-Level Marketing, Direct Selling, Network Marketing etc. A concerted drive by enforcement agencies with a meticulous plan supported by sensible legislations and mass movement alone can save the gullible public who fall victim to the fraud schemes. This alone will compel the fraud companies to accept the bare fact that to lie to people for extracting money is fraud, and is a form of theft.

The well orchestrated activities of the money chain companies which had swindled astronomical amount, the tentacles of which are spread even in the remote villages of the country, has become a social catastrophe. Unregulated investment schemes are posing serious threat to the economic fabric of several nations as a sizeable portion of their GDP is caught up in the Money Circulation Schemes, which does not create any additional value.

Economic Warfare

Economic warfare in the post-liberalization period is not confined to conventional methods till known to economists and law enforcing agencies alike. It cleverly manipulates merchandising into Multi-Level Marketing by fraudulent firms, pumps fake currency notes to sabotage foreign economies, and use information technology to suit their nefarious designs.

Injecting the virus of ponzi schemes into under-developed economies, which leads to continuous outflow of money into cross-boarder destinations is nothing but Economic Terrorism, because it opens a safe conduit for draining away the income and wealth of a country.

It may be a coincidence that majority of these companies are headquartered in America which is the hub of international finance capital. Meticulously designed economic crimes are used by the organized criminal gangs as a tool of illegitimate fund transfer. This has to be viewed from the perspective of international capital flight. The US companies like Amway, Avon Products Inc., Mery Kay Inc., Herba Life, Tupper Ware, Monavie etc. are all engaged in running either overt or covert chain referral business and are all the 'merchants of deception' and treachery.

Economic offenders are much ahead in their operations availing all the leaps in technology, which leaves even seasoned investigating officers awestruck. The machinations of these companies go beyond the known pastures of law enforcing agencies as it encompasses a variety of disciplines including economics, law, accounting, and information technology. The con men employ a number of tactics to hoodwink the investigations such as registering the firms in fake address, frequent changes in directorship, layering and de-layering of funds, laundering of funds for evading tracking, siphoning of funds through cross-boarder transfers and so on.

Fighting Economic Offences

This menace can be combated only with laws containing specific norms that are transparent, concrete, and intelligible, leaving no room for wrong interpretation. Stringent punitive measure will be a deterrent for those who think that they can fool the public with their "fantastic" schemes. A spate of discussion in the public domain on the ramifications of these schemes is inevitable to curb this.

It is high time that the policy makers in the country awakened to the stark reality that unless restrained, these companies will undermine the very fabric of our economy. The experience of the countries which witnessed the adverse macro-economic impact of devious investment schemes points to the need for early response from financial regulators and law enforcement authorities to identify, to stop the schemes and protect investors' interests.

Survival of any economy is rested on the investor's confidence in financial institutions. Undermining the confidence in the financial institutions and weakening the tools of monetary and fiscal policy will be the ultimate aftermath of these deceptive games. Swift response to this menace, tackling the social dimensions of the phenomenon and building a strong regulatory framework with effective supervision system are all the immediate tasks before the enforcement agency.

Behind the success stories of con men, there are innumerable instances of untold human miseries that include mass depression, mental illnesses, family breakups and even suicides. Those who invested their hard earned money expecting fabulous return have no choice but to end their lives once these schemes collapse. A cursory look at those who are knocking at the doors of judiciary for justice will amplify what has been said above. One can see hundreds of people who roam around after seeing the economic bubbles punctured.

The saddest part of the story is that the economists, politicians, government agencies and media unknowingly blow the trumpets for these con men. With the glossed up stories of a negligible minority who won the game, corporate lobby has succeeded in misleading a section in the society that their success is the result of "sheer entrepreneurship".

A close look at the economic, legal, ethical and business aspects of this looting has become imperative as these firms have been thriving on the ignorance of the public and the confusion among the law enforcing agencies. The words of W.B. Yeats "the best lack all convictions while the worst is full of passionate intensity"[5] passionately sum-up the impending danger that stares in the face of humanity. When the society is spinning out of control in the wake of the turmoil created by the mafia, the challenges of administration of criminal justice should go beyond the narrow purview of written law for meeting the fair ends of justice.

References

1. Kerala High Court: Kuriachan Chacko, Achamma Chacko and Linu Joy *vs.* State of Kerala 19/7/2007. Order of Kerala High Court, Justice Basant.
2. *Mein Kampf*, p. 134: Adolf Hitler.
3. *Merchants of Deception*—Eric Sheilbeier.
4. *Death of a Salesman*: American Playwright Arthur Miller.
5. W.B. Yeats: *Second Coming*.

2
Money Circulation Scheme as a Global Economic Crime

How would you earn six digit incomes per month, without much educational qualification? Asked a networking trainer to a group of wide eyed aspirants at a grooming business meet. MLM (Multi-Level Marketing) is the answer given by him and he wanted to give a magical introduction to his nefarious plan. Thefts by deception which takes the form of ponzi schemes, pyramid schemes and Multi-Level Marketing are lucrative to the criminal minds as the dividends involved is much higher than any other crimes or legal business. The proceeds of crime are beyond imagination.

There is an absolute reign of anarchy in several economies where the legal framework is fragile with no effective tool for taming deceptive investment schemes. A cursory glance of major incidents of corporate frauds by companies in different countries the world-over will give an understanding of the ramifications of the issue in terms of its volume and impact.

The adverse macro-economic impact is worse in the countries where the regulatory mechanism is fragile. Albania and Caribbean countries like Columbia and Lesotho have witnessed the most devastating and virulent manifestations caused by the puncture of economic bubbles. Several collective investment schemes run by big companies collapsed one by one, siphoning off the earnings of large mass of people. Their economy crumbled and faced the inevitable aftermath of financial and socio-political damage.

Albania

The volume of fund channelized through pyramid scheme in Albania expressed as a proportion of their national income is alarming. At their peak, it amounted to almost half of country's GDP. About two-third of the population invested in the get rich schemes. "The investment funds felt pressured to compete and began to offer higher interest rates on deposits. In July, Kamberi, (which run a pyramid scheme) raised its monthly interest rate to 10 per cent. In September, Populli (another company), began offering more than 30 per cent a month. In November, Xhafferi offered to treble depositors' money in three months; Sude responded with an offer to double principal in two months. By November, the face value of the schemes' liabilities totalled $1.2 billion. Albanians sold their houses to invest in the schemes; farmers sold their livestock. The mood is vividly captured by a resident who said that, in the fall of 1996, Tirana smelled and sounded like a slaughterhouse, as farmers drove their animals to market to invest the proceeds in the pyramid schemes."[1]

Several of these companies had no real assets. Ruling politicians were blamed for endorsing the scheme by repeatedly appearing in the functions of the Companies including VEFA Holding Group, an International Company which had branches in Germany and Italy.

Hell broke loose in Albania when the schemes collapsed unable to withstand their own wait. Albania descended into anarchy following a civil war like situation. Nearly 2000 people were killed in the city of Jarvis.[2]

There was complete chaos by March 1997. Army and Police members have deserted and gradually the government lost control. Million weapons were looted from the armouries. Customs posts and tax offices were burnt. Government was deprived of the revenue source. Albanean currency Lek, depreciated against American dollar by 40 per cent and hyper inflation weakened the economy. Trade and industries decayed. Finally, the government fell. All these were the socio-political fallout of the dubious investment schemes.

Columbia

Columbia is another example of how unchecked investment schemes will lead to unforeseen bedlam in the economy. The number of companies which run ponzi schemes on a competitive offer of returns were nearly 200 in the country. Most of these companies, in which thousands of people invested their life time earning, collapsed by the middle of 2008.

DRFE was a Spanish scheme which offered "Direct, Fast and Easy money", promising 300 per cent return within 6 months. People from poor background to high profile businessmen and politicians and even government councils found the investment scheme attractive. In the hope of doubling their investments within a short period, people even sold their houses for raising funds to invest in the collective schemes. Some of them even quit their job to become the promoter of the company. The scheme collected 1 billion dollars which is 0.4 per cent of GDP.

"Dear investors, thanks for trusting us and depositing your money," said a note on the door of a company in the province of Cauca. "Now, for being stupid and believing in financial witchcraft, you will have to work for your money."[3]

Police arrested two loan managers while trying to flee out of an investment office through the backdoors with four suitcases filled with cash. Rioting started as news spread that the owners of DRFE were arrested. It unleashed storms of protests. Thirteen Columbian cities witnessed violent outbursts of rioting by November 2008.[4] Enraged investors looted the company's offic. ind went on rampage in cities across Columbia. They looted and set ablaze the shops in the streets. Government buildings were attacked and two persons died in the riot.

Columbia's Chief Financial Regulator resigned. Government declared "Social Emergency". The punishments for such scams were hiked from six months to 20 years. So far, 92.4 billion pesos ($42m) have been seized from the DRFE offices, though officials believe the company may have taken as much as $200m in deposits.

Strangely Columbia also witnessed protest march against the enforcement agency as they believed that the authorities are spoiling their chances of making easy money. Such was the brainwashing of the Scamsters who instilled confidence in the investors by hook and crook even when the schemes were crumbling down. The people believed that the companies were "the banks of the poor". Sooner they became wary of even the legitimate banks and started keeping their savings under the mattress exacerbating the crisis.

Grupo DMG

Grupo DMG, a Columbian company named after its founder David Murcia Guzman, was one of the largest con schemes in the world.

DM Guzman's childhood was in abject poverty. He scrubbed the floor of restaurant to make a living. After dropping out from the school, he became a door-to-door salesman in a multi-level marketing (MLM) company. Seeing the immense opportunity of accumulation he opened his own MLM firm DMG.

Like any other MLM, the scheme flourished very fast in the initial days. Very soon the scheme spread to Venezuela and Ecuador. The scheme is a chain referral system which worked through credit cards distributed to investors. The card could be used to buy appliances and consumer electronics from selected retailers. Customers could also collect points which could be redeemed for cash after several months. The scheme offered a return of 150–300 per cent on investment. Customers also became salesmen. It remained current on its obligations for three years.

As the head of DMG, he reportedly lived a lavish life, with a private jet, and a fleet of expensive cars. Emerging from Bogota's Slums, later he dined and wined the provincial governors, flew to different cities aboard in his jet.

DMG allegedly provided financial support to political campaigns. According to law enforcement authorities, a taped conversation indicates that DMG sets aside US$ 322,000 to obtain parliamentary support for a law beneficial to DMG and also sought to buy favourable media coverage.

It evolved from a simple pyramid scheme into a sophisticated investment plan and there were 200,000 clients. Although this company had not stopped paying its clients even when other schemes collapsed, the government and prosecutors perused it further. The authorities later found out that the money they made out of drug trade was pumped into the scheme to withstand.

Police closed down 59 offices of DMG Grupo Holding. His arrest was followed by popular outrage and scandal involving political leaders and officials. Columbian President's chair trembled.

New York Times reported Where Officials See Fraud, Columbia's Masses see a Folk Hero in him. Some of the promoters went on hunger strike demanding his release as they believed the government intervention caused the loss of their savings.

"There was a twist to this Icarus like story. Many of the small investors in DMG saw Mr. Murcia not as a swindler but as their Savior and protested in capture in almost a dozen cities."[5]

OLINT Corporation

David Smith, a Jamaican national founded the corporation Overseas Locket International, in Panama. It served as a counsel for an investors' club for trading in foreign exchange. He had the experience of working as the licensed representative of another firm Jamaica Money Market Brokers Limited. He formed the investors club with his friends and other members in the firm began operation in the year 2004. He started foreign exchange trading rising funds from the members after offering an average of 10 per cent return per month. New members had to be referred by existing members who were paid a referral commission.

The fund he raked went beyond US$ 220 million from over 6000 investors. Gradually the Financial Service Commission (FSC) in Jamaica put the company under surveillance and made public warnings against it. Despite this money continued to flow into OLINT *via* feeder clubs.[6]

At the peak of its fame, David Smith was hailed as one of the greatest foreign exchange traders. OLINT supported political parties in Jamaica. The members of the club were mainly politicians, leading money market experts, doctors, and lawyers.

Errol Ennis, former Finance Minister, described the raid, on OLINT at the time, as a vulgar abuse of power by the state. Audley Shaw, the then Finance Minister said that FSC's actions against OLINT, which offers good interest rates, were unacceptable. Enforcement everywhere is like this. Without understanding the ramifications of the scheme even the Ministers make irresponsible statements which create rage among the investors against the enforcement agency.

OLINT sponsored the 2008 Jazz and Blue Festival. Former heads of the FSC, Byran Wynter, who became the governor of the Bank of Jamaica and George Roper the acting head 2007-2008, took much heat from the public for their strident opposition to the unregistered and unregulated financial operators.

Several other schemes, such as Lew Fam, appeared to be conduits for OLINT. It collected nearly 2 billion which is nearly 12 per cent of the GDP of the nation. After operating on a world-wide platform the scheme finally perished, draining away the hard earned money of millions. Now the founder, David Smith is sentenced to 30 years of imprisonment and is languishing in jail.

Cash Plus Limited

Carlos Hill, another Jamaican national who had worked in the financial sector in the United States in the 1980s, founded the company Cash Plus Limited. The Swiss debenture scheme run by the company Cash Plus is later on found to be a ponzi scheme and it duped the investors to the tune of US$ 326 million.

An exorbitant interest of 10 per cent per month is paid to the investors, and the lender could redeem the principal after 10 months. Cash Plus began operations as early as 2002 and operated up to 2008 in Greneda. Carlos Hill was finally arrested in 2009. This was followed by protest march in major cities under the auspices of the promoters. 30 million people fell victim to the scam.[7]

The SEC has filed an emergency action in federal court in New Jersey to halt the scheme and is criminally charged in Jamaica. It was exposed in 2008. The case was a subject of hot debate internationally. Operations to unearth the fund siphoned off by the company extended to Caribbean countries, Europe and Dubai. The Securities and Exchange Commission of US levied a fine of $5,000 against Hill.

MKM Burial Society in Lesotho was launched as a firm licensed to undertake Funeral in Lesotho. It was funded with public contributions. Gradually, it started underwriting of insurance business. Later, it started the Star Lion Gold Coin Investment Scheme during 2007 offering 60 per cent per year. Through the scheme, the company defrauded 42 million, i.e. 3 per cent of GDP and nearly 100,000 people fell victim to the scheme.

The schemes by the companies TAT savings spread in Macedonia, Caritas in Romania, MMM in Russia and CLAE in Peru, Defiment Bank in Serbia are all the examples of billion dollar chain referral scams with the total fund raised through the scheme going up to double digit in terms of the percentage of national income.

In the African countries Pyramid Schemes camouflaged as co-operative societies in the last phase of their operations. The hue and cry from the public following the fall of HYIPS one by one lead to the formation of a Special Task Force in 2009. The task force identified 270 pyramid and other related schemes with 148,784 investors who have invested a total sum of Kshs. 8,178,737,402.

"The Central Bank of Kenya issued press notices in February and May 2007 urging the public against investing in pyramid schemes. These statements were negatively received by the public who viewed them as government interference to otherwise legitimate investments."[8]

Challenge to Developed Economies

Even developed countries which claim to have strong regulatory mechanisms are not exceptions to this pervasive and persistent virus of money circulation schemes.

US have managed to take a dual stand on the issue with a system of red flag to the investors to identify the fraud schemes within the domestic economy. At the same time, it extracts fund from the under-developed capital markets through covert money circulation schemes. The adverse macro-economic impact within the country is negligible.

During 2008-2012, State Economic Commission could effectively intervene and court orders were obtained against a series of Ponzi schemes. The collections of three of these companies went beyond US$ 300 each. The attachment orders were issued against all these. Out of this the case of one Norman Hsu who raised $60 million, attracted the world during 2008, as the allegations of heavy contributions to prominent politicians came out.

Developed world is the epicenter of several schemes which spread internationally extracting money from the backward economies. Hundreds of firms registered in America, promote fraudulent schemes, running covert money circulation schemes, hidden behind marketing. Any interception in these schemes in foreign countries by enforcement agencies are taken up in diplomatic level.

Bernard Madoff Investment Securities LLC

Ponzi scheme run by Bernard Madoff which swindled US$ 50 billion, in the United States is a recent example of how the fraudsters pose a serious challenge even to the developed economies. Madoff scheme operated in United States during 2008. Bernad Madoff was a prominent member in American securities industry. He was a high profile investment adviser registered at the Securities and Exchange Commission. He served on the board and in leadership positions of both the National Association of Securities Dealers and the NASDAQ Stock Market.

Madoff floated a firm named Bernard Madoff Investment Securities (BMIS), and launched an investment scheme offering high guaranteed return. An amount of nearly US$ 50 billion was collected. This was proved to be the largest investment fraud ever committed. When the scheme crashed, criminal investigation was initiated. Madoff had confessed that he was running a Ponzi scheme for many years using the investment adviser status of the firm.

The firm's purported investment strategy consisted of purchasing blue chip stocks and taking option contracts on them. He never undertook those transactions. His fund offered attractive and unusually steady returns to an exclusive clientele, consisting of prominent Jewish executives and organizations. It offered yearly return of 20 per cent and the volume of fraud is nearly 50 billion dollars which is 0.3 per cent of GDP. Nearly 13,000 people fell victim to the fraud scheme and lost their money.[9]

Financial analysts had given credible and specific warning and red flags on the scheme well in advance and this was ignored by the SECs. After initial hesitation, civil action and criminal investigations are initiated. Subsequently, US court had frozen all the assets of Madoff in civil proceedings. On December 11, 2008, the SEC brought emergency actions in the district court, alleging violations of the United States securities laws. A total cumulative punishment of 150 years of rigorous imprisonment was awarded by the judicial court.

In the civil proceedings he had consented to pay off the liabilities, penalties and prejudgment interest without admitting or denying the allegations.

BMIS was liquidated at the initiative of the Securities Investor Protection Corporation (SIPC) and the assets were distributed to customers and other claimants by the SIPC trustee. The investigator, DJ Sheefan wrote "A Ponzi scheme the size and duration of Bernard Madoff's was only possible if he went global. The magnitude of his financial fraud still holds the world record, with approximately $17.5 billion in losses. Four years of investigation has revealed that Madoff's Ponzi scheme is unprecedented in its global reach—our work reconstructing the fraud has taken us into more than 30 jurisdictions to date."[10]

Peter Sander gives a compelling reading of how Madoff evolved himself from a penny stockist to the covetous rank of Vice President of New York Stock Exchange and the manager of big funds.[11]

Even the socialist countries are not exceptions to the greed ruling the market. *Shangai Daily* reports the arrest of hundreds of MLM Promoters and freezing of nearly 67 Million Yuan in Bank accounts. Chinese government promulgated a new legislation against the Pyramid Investment Schemes with deterrent provisions to prosecute the promoters.

One company, named MMM, running pyramid schemes literally created tremors in the Russian economy. European Union also faced the bad impact of market saturation caused by the MLM companies. German court has recently convicted the Multi National Company Herbalife.

Despite these experiences companies running devious schemes are mushrooming in all the countries. It poses a real challenge to enforcement agencies and legislators.

The reluctance of the enforcement agencies to intercept the schemes, Promoters taking out open protest marches against arrest of fraudsters, political leaders and ministers coming out with open statements defending the fraud etc. can be attributed to the inadequate understanding of the programmes due to its sophisticated nature. Even when the scheme comes to the radar of investigators they fear any interference will trigger sudden collapse. Companies will attribute the liquidity crisis to government intervention rather than the inherent flaws of the scheme. Operators of many schemes have managed to extend their operations by showy charitable contributions, significant political contributions, and pompous demonstrations of their own wealth.

Public Relations Programme

For obtaining media support and for manipulating public opinion, very sensitive public relations campaigns involving donations to charitable cause and sponsorship of high profile events are resorted to by the companies.

- Cash Plus began a three-year sponsorship of the Jamaican National Premier League soccer at J$50 million per year, since September 2007.
- OLINT has donated US$ 1 million to its charitable foundation to help deprived children. It also sponsored the 2008 Air Jamaica Jazz and Blues Festival. It was reported that both of the main Jamaican political parties received campaign donations from OLINT.
- Another scheme has sponsored the Jamaican entry in the Miss Universe beauty pageant in January 2008.
- The MMM scheme in Russia financed the 1994 World Cup soccer team.
- David Smith, the founder of OLINT was named as the Business Personality of the Year by a newspaper.[12]

In Albania, even when the schemes starting crumbling down, government was supporting the companies. Frequent functions were held by the companies with the senior government officials as chief guest. The prime minister and the speaker were accused for accepting medal at the anniversary meeting of one company. Heavy contributions were given to the senior politicians for campaigning during 1996 election.

These experiences point to immense danger to the society if authorities fail to curb the menace in the bud. Lethargic and indolent approach on the part of the enforcement agencies in rising to the occasion with sharp policy response will have the aftermath of violent outbusts of protests. Early detection and successfull prosecution and initiating civil proceedings require a better understanding of the ramifications of the schemes.

Though most of the swindling techniques originated long back, the application of computer and internet adds new dimension to these. The sham sites of the fraudsters create an image that their company is a large and reputed one and for this they provide links of government departments and other legitimate sites.

The tentacles of money circulation schemes, spread across the world, drain away the hard earned money of the public and it has become a social catastrophe in almost all the countries. This calls forth a detailed theoretical analysis of various business models offered by the fraud companies to expose its unviability.

The archetype of money circulation schemes originated in the form of Ponzi schemes before 1950s, gradually developed into more overt Pyramid schemes in 1990s and now it takes the form of camouflaged, Multi-Level Marketing and insurance policy premium linked MLM. These are all outright thefts and cheating as investor's money is returned in none of these schemes.

References

1. *The Rise and Fall of Albania's Pyramid Schemes*: Christopher Jarvis.
2. *Ibid.*
3. Columbia, Tumbling Pyramids: *The Economist.*
4. *The Guardian*, Friday 14 November, 2008.
5. *New York Times*, January 30, 2009. Where Officials See Fraud, Columbia's Masses see a folk Hero: By Simon Romero.
6. Olint Ponzi's Boss David Smith gets 30 years: posted by 'investor life'.
7. IMF Working Paper: Ponzi Schemes in the Caribbean: Ana Carvajal, Hunter Monroe, Catherine Pattillo, and Brian Wynter.
8. Report of the Taskforce on Pyramid Schemes, Republic of Kenya—Ministry of Co-operative Development and Marketing.
9. Bernard Madoff Fast Facts by CNN Library, April 16, 2013.
10. A Message from the SIPA Trustee's Chief Counsel, David J. Sheehan, November 7, 2012.
11. Peter J. Sander: Madoff: Corruption, Deceit, and the Making of the World's Most Notorious Ponzi Scheme.
12. IMF Working Paper: Ponzi Schemes in the Caribbean: Ana Carvajal, Hunter Monroe, Catherine Pattillo, and Porian Wynter.

3
Investment Scams—Indian Scenario

India's Consumer Market

India, with its mammoth population and strong social networks, offers unlimited scope for the scamsters running chain recruitment who invade the economy like swarms of locusts. There has been unprecedented spurt in the activities of dubious firms that eye on the vast market available in India.

As one MLM company observed, "The country has an abundant supply of manpower. Indians like to maintain strong social network". The companies find India as an ideal destination because their working mechanism rely much on the potential of a member to bring in his friends and family members within the ambit of endless chain of salesmen.

The scope of Indian consumer market and the shift in consumption pattern is rightly assessed by the multinational MLM companies. "In 2007, India was ranked the 12th largest consumer market in the world and it is expected to be the fifth largest consumer market by 2025 after the United States (US), Japan, China and the United Kingdom (UK)."[1]

Towards the midst of 90s Amway entered Indian domestic market and their fanciful schemes were immediately duplicated by large number of Indian companies. Subsequently, many foreign companies, which neither bring in any foreign direct investment nor promote any technology transfer, were also allowed access to Indian consumer market camouflaging as direct selling firms. Soon they started running money circulation schemes under the garb of product sales.

Globalization and Corporate Fraud

Though low profile money chain operations with small stakes operated in India long ago, it was the integration of Indian domestic economy to the world market as part of globalization that opened the floodgates to several foreign firms that started to prowl on the Indian soil. It led to globalization of crimes and flourishing of corporate frauds resulting in a continuous draining of funds to the foreign destinations.

There are nearly 13 lakh registered companies in India and not less than 12,000 companies are being registered every year. Most of the MLM companies do not file annual returns as they wind up their activities within four or five months after registration. The businesses being carried out by these companies normally go beyond the apparent objectives that are stated in the memorandum and articles of association. There is no mechanism for checking as to whether the companies cross the legal border.

It may be recalled that SEBI had identified 669 companies whose operations amount to violation of the SEBI Act. As many as 552 companies have been prosecuted and conviction was secured in 124 cases. The amount collected by these companies from the public was about Rs. 7435 crore.[2]

Financial Professional Turns Unethical

Despite the arrest of several computer engineers in different cases registered in various states for providing software support to MLM companies, large number of MLM software supporting companies are still operating in the country which provide technical as well as consultancy service for the running of MLM schemes. Their website exhibits the name of hundreds of MLM companies across the countries as their clients.

To make matters worse, chartered accountants too become key players in the game. Many of them get a percentage of company's turn over as reward for their service. The service of the accountants are not limited to offering advises to the company owners. There are instances of the accountants later becoming the agents of the MLM companies.

Sensing the possibility of huge returns, the auditors of MLM companies later start their own ventures. Dharmendra Kottari, a trainee auditor for Inway Marketing, later became the CEO for a company named Red Carpet Entertainment Pvt. Ltd., which was running pyramid scheme. He then floated another company named Lakshya India Marketing Pvt. Ltd. RBI issued directives to keep the operation of these companies under surveillance. So many other auditors also turned into owners of MLM companies.[3]

Bank managers too fail to meet their social and legal responsibility under pressure of achieving deposit targets. If a deposit of Rs. one crore is offered anybody can start account anywhere in India, violating the norms of "Know Your Customer" issued by the Apex Bank. MLM offers lot of liquidity to the banks as it deals with continuous cash flow. When the deposits of MLM companies are frozen by the investigating officers, it is generally kept with banks and is utilized by them. Huge amounts in the accounts of Fine India, Lakshya India, RMP, Stock Guru etc. are blocked in the banks. Huge amount is charged by the advocates for the de-freezing suits.

Misrepresentations by the Companies

'Legal opinion' of former chief justice of India on MLM companies is exhibited in the site of MLM companies to add credibility to their business. It is a growing trend on the part of the companies to cite opinion of retired justices, favouring their claims. Supreme Court has expressed serious concern over this development.

MLM companies flaunt the opinion of a former Chief Justice in their petitions filed in many cases. However, it did not cut much ice with the Supreme Court when Amway filed; a Special Leave petition against the judgment of Andhra Pradesh High Court. Now after the Supreme Court passed a judicial order barring such opinions, these crooks like Amway, *et al.* could no longer annex their petitions with the opinions of former chief justices.[4]

The companies running pyramid schemes approach the High Court with claim that they are engaged in product sales and Court will grant interim directions such as "Police shall not interfere in the lawful business activity". This will be exhibited in the websites of the company as approval from the Court. The general direction in the writ petition is not binding on the enforcement agency as the running of Money Circulation Scheme is not lawful Business Activity.

Collective investment schemes resort to large scale misinterpretation of court directives. The most dangerous of all these is the claim that MLM is legal and sanction is given by the Central Government for running the scheme. Such claims can be seen in the websites of many companies engaged in MLM.

Permission given by the Foreign Investment Promotion Board to AMWAY for doing selling and that too for bringing Foreign Direct Investment is misrepresented as the sanction of Central Government for conducting money circulation scheme. Likewise a letter from Consumer Affairs Ministry is misinterpreted to be the sanction for product based MLM. RBI have warned that the individuals, firms and unincorporated bodies who collect money through illegal money circulation scheme does not have the approval of the apex bank.

Direct Marketing Trade Unions

Clear and specific judgements have come from the Honourable Supreme Court and various High Courts, highlighting the illegality of Multi-Level Marketing. But this has not prevented by the MLM companies to get the employees in the segment united under the banner of trade unions sponsored by political parties. The companies use the collective bargaining power of the trade unions to shield their illegal business. The trade unions even resort to open agitations for the cause of the MLM companies without understanding the entire ramifications of the treachery.

Nearly 2000 domestic companies are running either overt money circulation schemes or hidden multi-level marketing. The employees and promoters of these companies constitute a large influential segment in the society. The political parties which eye on the vote bank in the community intervene when the enforcement agencies crack the whip. It is mutually beneficial agreement for both the parties because the politicians get the large chunk of the MLM junkies into the trade union and the companies get political power to protect them from legal action. There were instances when political parties insisted on joining their trade unions when they were approached by the MLM companies for shelter.

A number of mysterious organizations have been sprouted in India, many of which pose itself as the protectors of consumers right. They organized huge rallies, hold hunger strikes and use all democratic means to exert pressure on the governments. Most of these unions claim that their aim is to protect direct selling which is legally permissible. In effect the illegal system of sale of product at inflated prices through an endless chain of recruiters which exploit the end consumers are defended by these trade unions.

State Governments initiate modifications of rule and ambiguous guidelines which gives chance to the illegal ventures to present the scheme as legitimate. Reluctance on the part of the enforcement agencies, except in a few states, to take firm legal action led to flourishing of these schemes.

References

1. *Socio-economic Impact of Direct Selling—Need for a Policy Stimulus*, Arpitha Mukharjee, Thanu M. Goyal, Divya Stija, Nirupama Soundararajan.
2. *Economic Times*: 5.5.13.
3. RBI 2009-10/158. UBD.CO.BPD Cir. No 5/12.05.2001./2009-10, September 16/2009.
4. Corporate Fraud Watch 4.2.2012.

4
Economics of Money Circulation Schemes

The illusory world of gambling is better illustrated in the epic Mahabharata which is the story of the great Kurukshetra war, born out of a game of dice between Yudhisthira and Sakuni. The fierce insanity of gambler is seen in Yudhisthira playing dice pledging even his wife in anticipation of winning, after losing his palace, kingdom, servants and brothers.

Dostoevsky's 'The Gambler' is the story of a man who is psychologically addicted to Gambling, who desperately keep on playing even after repeated losses.[1] Motivated by the desire of 'getting rich quick', the gamblers go on chasing the mirage and gradually develop a harmful behavioural disorder.

In the modern period gaming takes several dimensions ranging from betting on dice to the billion dollar money circulation scheme. Commercial gambling is a multi-crore industry in the world and it manifests in the form of instant lotteries, casino table games, electronic gaming machines in clubs and wagering on races and sport events. The advent of computer and internet connected the gamblers the world- over and this made electronic gambling a high profile industry.

Circulation of Money without Value Addition

Gambling is wagering of money or valuable thing, in anticipation of an income, on an event of uncertain outcome which can be known within a short term. A participant can gain in a gambling only at the loss of another and thus these are zero sum games. There is no net gain as the gain of the winner cannot be greater than the loss of the loser. There is no value addition in the process of a gambling and this is only rotating of money from one pocket to another. It simply circulates money among participants and does not create new wealth.

Before attaining the final form, a manufactured product goes through several stages and there is value addition in each stage. The market price of the product is the sum of all these value additions. Any process which is devoid of a value addition cannot be considered an economic activity.

Nobel Laureate Paul Samuelson observes "Gambling involves simply sterile transfers of money or goods between individuals, creating no new money or goods. Although it creates no output, gambling does nevertheless absorb time and resources. When pursued beyond the limits of recreation, where the main purpose after all is to kill time, gambling subtracts from the national income."[2]

Pyramid Scheme and MLM as Gambling

The money circulation schemes including Ponzi scheme, pyramid scheme and MLM are all gambling in the sense that it is rotating fund among the members without any value addition and thus it is a sheer waste of time and energy. The companies running investment schemes based on pyramid model enrollment of investors cannot divert the fund to any productive channel, as working mechanism of this sly game is to make exorbitant pay outs to senior members.

An element of gambling is present in money circulation schemes to some extent because they are also a zero sum game. It creates a psychological addiction to the participants and the victims are the willing participants in the game. Large majority will lose money when the pyramid collapses.

It is a more cruel game as the direction of transfer of fund is only from bottom to top and all the members do not have a chance of winning. It goes beyond gambling in the traditional sense as the dominant feature is the application of deceptive tools of cheating and outright theft. The wallets of the gullible public are looted by the companies by making tall false claims and offers.

The purchase of products by a member in an MLM, in anticipation of the commission he is going to get while an endless chain of downline sellers enroll under him is only a gambling table behaviour of an addictive game.

Those who enroll in money circulation schemes also make subjective evaluation of the probable earning and this influences their consumption pattern.

Though, these are presented as income opportunities and high yielding business, it is not at all an economic activity. These are nefarious games designed to pilfer the earning of the public. In another perspective, it can be seen that only greedy and gullible indulge in the rat race in their crazy pursuit of acquisition and fall prey to these schemes. Gullibility in this context cannot be differentiated from criminality and thus the act of joining in money circulation schemes are defined as criminal offence in the law of all the nations.

Gambling Behaviour in Money Chain

Gaming options of the individuals are explained by economists in different ways. The spending of time and money without any rational evaluation is considered as simply myopic consumption out of psychological addictions. What drives the participant to gambling is not just the pecuniary gain. Even the participation becomes an enjoyable experience and habit forming ingredient.

Gambling is explained by some economists using the concept of economic surplus, i.e., even the decision to gamble is economically rational as they try to maximise the benefits basing on a subjective evaluation of the benefit and cost of their decision.

Barker and Britz acknowledge gambling to be a deviant behaviour which needs to be controlled by legislation.[3] Explaining the metamorphosis of the concept of gambling over the years, they argued that gambling was considered to be a sin and crime in the older days. But, it has become more or less a legal activity in modern period.

Gambling: Who Wins? Who Lose[4] compiled by Gerda Reith, assesses the social costs and benefits of gambling. It is a collection of articles reviewing the impact of gambling from the legal, economic, political, psychological, social, and ethical perspectives.

Becker and Murphy[5] came forward with the theory of rational addiction, denouncing the concept that addicts are myopic consumers. According to them, people who indulge in habit forming and addictive gambling do make rational calculations and respond to changes in economic parameters. Becker and Murphy say that it is wrong to assume that problem gamblers are incapable of taking consistent decisions. The theory of rational addiction postulates that the gamblers have a consistent plan to maximize utility over time. Addiction is the impact of past consumption of the good on current consumption.

Later, economists like Ole Rogebergyz[6], unleashed scathing attack on the theory of Rational addiction, asking the question: How can economists take absurd theories of choice seriously? The theory was alleged to be one based on wrong assumptions, psychologically persuasive stories and poorly anchored mathematical models.

Though not much attention is paid by the academics on the socio-economic impact of money circulation schemes, studies are galore on the ill effects of gambling. A study in Australia undertakes the in-depth analysis of the impact of gambling from economist's, sociologist's and psychologist's angle.[7]

If alcoholism, drug addiction depression and suicide are the outcome of gambling, the impact of so called collective investment schemes is deeper and manifold. It pushes a large section of the society to live in an unreal world that has its own logic and dynamism. They make calculations of the prospective income and make castles in the air. It would take some time for them to realize fallacies and follies but by then they might have reached a point of no return. Mass depression, rioting and suicides are the visible signs of the malady.

It has been observed that passionate pursuers of MLM and pyramid scheme share some of the characteristics of the persons suffering from psychic disorders. Glued to the screens of computers for hours, they keenly observe the expansion of the network under them and devising strategies to place the new entrants at suitable places. The care they take in positioning a new member in the right place is akin to the thought process of a chess player before making a move.

Not much credence can be given to the subjective calculations of individual members of money circulation scheme as these are far-fetched and divorced from reality. Though, there may be attempts to maximize the individual utility based on rational behaviours, the net impact is only negative in respect of this gambling. Analysis of the individual costs and benefits is only futile intellectual exercise as the negative macro-economic impact is beyond imagination.

The element of gambling is predominant in money chain operations and only those who take it as a sly game make gain out of it. Those who innocuously invest in these firms, mistaking it as a genuine investment option, are bound to be doomed. The senior leaders who are in the know of the inner dynamics of the game shift from one scheme to another after bargaining with the companies. They also take along with them the entire downline network to the new companies that offer them bounties.

The professional gamblers in Money Circulation Scheme developed this acumen as a tool to find good fortunes for themselves. Those who know how to make a move at right time inside the company and to make the call outside decide the fate of schemes. But the unsuspecting herd of downline members who migrate from one company to another does not gain much from the transition.

Contrary to the public perception, downing the shutters of a firm need not be a negative thing for the owners. Sometimes, they deliberately dismantle the whole operation when it reaches the optimum point where the margin between earning and payout is the maximum. There is a point from where carrying forward with the scheme anymore will lead to a fall in the accumulated income of the company. Even registering of case is taken as golden chance for winding up the operation and to blame the enforcement agency for their failure to make further payments.

Social impact assessment of money chain schemes have unravelled that many a psychic problems faced by the problem gamblers are applicable to the MLM junkies also.

Socio-Economic Impact of Money Circulation Schemes

In most cases those who invest in the collective investment schemes looses everything are returned and it amounts to outright theft. Schemes such as Pyramid and MLM are more complex with even the victims justifying the cause of the scamsters.

Poor economies are less capable of surviving the damages caused by the collapse of the investment schemes without socio-political impacts.

Pyramid schemes plague the financial market and it spoil the economic fabric of the country. The working mechanism of the scheme is built on the fluid and arithmetically infeasible foundations. These are unworkable and are only tall false claim to induce people to part with their hard earned money. As the scheme spreads downwards, it requires recruiting new members at a geometrically expanding rate.

Market saturation, organizational problem caused by the pyramid structure of investors and even the morality and ethics of the greedy craze of investors are all the grounds on which ponzi schemes as well as multi level marketing is objected.

An economy can be plundered by a foreign company by injecting a money circulation scheme and the life blood of the economy will be drained away through the endless outward flow of money. Despite the prosecution being faced the worldover, the multinational fraud firms are making annual turnover of billions.

The most devastating effects of the frauds manifests in people going for borrowing loans from banks, and other Institutions to invest in the chain referral scheme. Even instances of people diverting their life time saving and retirement benefits to the "high yielding investment schemes" and even resorting to sell their assets to make investments in the schemes are experienced by the investigating officers.

Large-scale negative economic consequences of the scheme include:

- Undermining confidence in financial markets; diverting savings from productive to unproductive uses and, in some cases, from the domestic economy to foreign destinations, with a balance of payments impact;
- When the asset bubble is punctured, there is a sudden fall in the perceived wealth. As the bubble expands, seeing the large downline network imagination of future income shoot up the sky. Pseudo income shown in the E-wallet and paper profit makes the members feel better off than they actually are. This changes their consumption patter their demand for goods and money increases. This causes swings in consumption and accelerates inflation. Once the bubble bursts, perceived wealth falls dramatically. Demana for goods and money, as well as output and inflation rates, can be expected to decrease.

- When large group of households thrown to unforeseen losses suddenly, it causes socio-economic strife. Civil disorder creates the most damaging effects. The social effects were profound. In addition to the loss of life, thousands of people were impoverished either by their unwise investments in the pyramid schemes or by the destruction of their property in the ensuing violence. The pyramid scheme phenomenon was a sobering setback.[8]
- Undermining the reputation of political authorities, regulators, and law enforcers for failing to prevent open frauds. Loss of credibility and a tainted image of this group will have far reaching ramifications on the very existence of the democratic polity.

Adverse Impact on Banking Sector

Banking sector will be the worst affected when the High Yielding Investment Programmes are not regulated as it diverts funds from banks. Experience of several countries shows that when these schemes proliferate, there will be a large increase in non-performing loans of banks as loan proceeds are normally pooled into these schemes. Loan delinquencies are the phenomenon whereby the investors turn unable to meet their repayment liabilities.

A seminar was organized under the auspices of the World Bank in Washington in the year 2008, on the "Schemes Affecting Banking Systems" for warning the economists, legislators and police officials the worldover to keep vigil against these schemes. Another seminar on "Understanding and Combating Unregulated Investment Schemes" also addressed the same issue.

Still almost all the fraudulent schemes are run through the banking network. The collection of deposit and disbursement of payouts are done through NEFT or RTGS. Despite specific guidelines and directives from the apex bank, the lukewarm approach of the bankers indirectly connive the offences. Banks cannot be silent spectators when deposits are piling in the accounts opened in fake addresses violating the 'Know Your Customer' norms. Failure of banks to meet their social and legal obligations finally culminates in siphoning of funds by fraudsters.

The commercial banks are to show diligence in identifying the accounts the deposits to which exhibit a pyramid schemes character. Deposits to such accounts are not to be accepted by the banks and should initiate legal action after freezing the account. Reserve Bank of India Act have clear provisions for this. This will be discussed in another chapter.

Layering and de-layering of funds, frequent changing of account operators, precautions to evade fund tracking are all the strange oddities of this new generation crime. Fraudsters have devised techniques to overcome the KYC norms and bulk transaction monitoring.

Normally, while executing a RTGS/NEFT transaction, bankers are supposed to collect beneficiary details mandatorily. Net banking system facilitates the bankers to do the transactions at the customer's level. Even if the customer has executed the fund transfer through net banking, they cannot add a beneficiary without inputting the details as per KYC norms. But these are overlooked by the bankers.

As a Tool of International Capital Flight

Capital flight from the domestic economy through illegitimate means is an acute economic problem being faced by the developing nations. It poses serious dearth of capital for the development. The main conduit of capital flight is through illegitimate business and trade mis-invoicing.

The extent of capital flight from the backward economies assumed alarming proportion in the recent years due to the spurt of money circulation scheme in various forms working on an international platform. Enormous funds are raised from the under-developed economies by the Transnational Companies running Pyramid schemes and MLM and these are taken to the cross-boarder destinations.

Money Circulation Schemes, spread internationally, leads to a drain of funds towards the originating country. When the scheme attracts foreign investors it can cause current account imbalance.

The current account of the balance of payments deteriorated to 9.1 per cent of GDP. Civil disorder led to a steep fall in production by about 7 per cent in 1997. Inflation rate went galloping to more than 40 per cent in 1997. Value of Albanian currency, lek, fell fiscal deficit increased sharply by the loss of government revenues during the period of civil disorder. Capital inflows declined.[9]

It will be further augmented by the consumption boom inspired by the inflated income perception of the consumers, based on anticipations of payouts. In Albania, there was a 35 per cent increase in imports following the consumption boom.

Besides, trade mis-invoicing, the capital earned through illegitimate business like money circulation schemes have become the main content of un-recorded outflow through clandestine routes. The study, "The Absorption of Illicit Financial Flows from Developing Countries: 2002-2006", shows the illicit outflow of trillions of dollars from the developing countries, as proceeds of crime, corruption, and tax evasion.[10]

Another study, "The Drivers and Dynamics of Illicit Financial Flows From India, 1948-2008", released by the Global Financial Integrity, an international agency that promotes national and multilateral policies, safeguards, and agreements aimed at curtailing the cross-border flow of illegal money, estimates that tax evasion, crime, and corruption have removed gross illicit assets from India worth US$ 462 billion.[11]

The access of large number of foreign companies doing MLM business into India, in the recent years fostered an underground economy that fuelled the outflow of capital from India. Indian companies who wanted to shift the huge funds raised through the swindling schemes to the tax havens also augmented this flow. The directors of these companies became High Net-Worth Individuals (HNWIs) who drive fund out of India's private sector to the offshore financial centres.

The greatest beneficiary of this capital flight is the United States as they get access to the worlds savings with the US$ being the global reserve currency. MLM companies augmented further flight of capital to the dollar as many of the world spread schemes are headquartered in the US.

The funds accumulated in the accounts of MLM companies are generally transferred to the accounts of these companies in the originating countries. This laundering process leads to Capital Flight. The savings of the Third World are propelled to the first through the private international banking and is largely denominated in the US$ and Swiss Franc.

Swiss International Private Banking website says: "Switzerland's celebrated insistence on banking secrecy protects all customers and their assets against access by non-authorized persons or official bodies, on the condition that the assets deposited do not originate from activities defined under Swiss Law as being of a criminal nature." Deutsche Bank's website on the internet boasts about its expansion of private banking in India as significant in its international operations. "In Asia we expanded our presence above all in India and Malaysia."

Riggs Bank, N.A., of Washington D.C., "offers a full range of international private banking services. Our International Service Banking office provides discreet, personalized, and specially adapted activities needed by prominent foreign customers…."[12]

Transnational Crime in the Developing World evaluates the overall size of criminal markets in 12 categories: drugs, humans, wildlife, counterfeit goods and currencies, human organs, small arms, diamonds and other gems, oil, timber, fish, art and cultural property, and gold. Of the 12 illicit activities studied, trade in drugs ($320 billion per year) and counterfeiting ($250 billion per year) are ranked first and second in terms of illicit funds generated. Study of fund transfers by the money chain companies will definitely outweigh these figures.

The co-operation of Banks in the global financial centres by sharing information among governments on all the suspicious transaction would become a great assistance in the detection and tracking of illicit financial flows. A conducive environment for Ponzi scheme is provided by the secrecy of bank transaction offered by the offshore middlemen.

Ponzi Scheme are mostly run by the companies under a holding company registered offshore with bank accounts. These overseas hideouts allow economic offenders to obscure the origins and destinations of the huge sums of cash. *Michael I. Goldberg*, expert on Ponzi schemes says "Very rarely do you have one that does not include offshore companies or accounts? If you don't, it's usually a very parochial, Podunk type of Ponzi. But the more sophisticated ones almost always do."

Allen Stanford's $7 billion fraud was run through a bank in Antugua. Bernard Madoff used a series of offshore feeder funds to fuel the growth of his $65 Billion house of cards. Three hedge funds from the Cayaman Islands was at the core of the fraud in the Illarramendi's Ponzi scheme.

The companies which operated in India like Qnet and Speak Asia have transferred very huge funds to their Singapore account. Other companies also shifted their funds to foreign bank branches when the investigating officers started freezing the accounts of the companies. Failure on the part of the new generation banks to block such transfers lead to drain of capital from the country.

A vibrant civil society and an independent media exposing financial crimes to the public scrutiny are the essential prerequisites for any fight against illegal capital flights related to this kleptocracy.

Stringent enforcement against MLM is called for in the wake of the tragic experience of countries where the high yielding investment schemes are not controlled. People would not lash out at the scheme as it comes as "income or business opportunity", but soon they vanishes with savings of large mass. More than 90 per cent of the people who participate in a pyramid investment scheme loses money wholly or partially, regardless of the stage at which it collapses. In a Product based Scheme this takes alarming magnitudes.

The business model of various forms of money circulation schemes requires a meticulous analysis and the proportion of members losing in the scheme as percentage of the total members can be explained with mathematical tools. This will be done in the ensuing chapters.

References

1. Fyodor Dostoevsky. '*The Gambler*'—the gaming hunger and the mania of gambling is depicted in the novel.
2. Paul, A. Samuelson, 1976, *Economics*, 10th ed., p. 425.
3. *Jokers Wild: Legalized Gambling in the Twenty-first Century* (Westport, CT: Praeger), editors Thomas Barker and Marjie Britz.
4. *Gambling. Who Wins? Who Loses? by Gerda Reith:* Amherst, NY: Prometheus Books, 2003.
5. *The Market for Illegal Goods: The Case of Drugs*—Gary S. Becker and Kevin M. Murphy, University of Chicago and Hoover Institution—Michael Grossman—City University of New York Graduate Centre and National Bureau of Economic Research.

6. " Taking Absurd Theories Seriously: Economics and the Case of Rational Addiction Theories"; Ole Rogebergyz.
7. Acil Tasman, Socio-Economic Impact of Gambling on the Northern Territory.
8. Social and Economic Impact Study into Gambling in Tasmania South Australian Centre for Economic Studies, Adelaide and Flinders Universities.
9. Christopher Jarvis, 1999, "The Rise and Fall of the Pyramid Schemes in Albania," *IMF Working Paper 99/98* (International Monetary Fund: Washington).
10. M. Rishi, and J.K. Boyce (1990), "The Hidden Balance-of-Payments: Capital Flight and Trade Misinvoicing in India, 1971-1986", *Economic and Political Weekly*, July, pp. 1645-48.
11. *http://india.gfip.org*
12. "Money Laundering and Capital Flight", Kannan Sreenivasan.

5
Ponzi Schemes

The Rise of Mr. Ponzi

Carlo Pietro Giovanni Guglielmo Tebaldo Ponzi, was a mythical figure who like a pied piper led millions of fortune seekers into a deceptive scheme which created an investment frenzy in America in 1920s. He was being followed by a money madding crowd wherever he went. When Ponzi said "Columbus and Marconi were greater. Columbus discovered America, Marconi discovered the wireless" the crowd thundered "But you discovered money!"[1]. Such was his persuasive power to drive the masses to money frenzy.

Who was this man and what was the black magic he wielded? The man whose name has become synonymous with wild speculation in money market has become the archetype of all the deceptive investments schemes. Ponzi scheme is named after the Italian godfather Charles **Ponzi.** He was born in Italy in 1882, devised some deceptive schemes through which unimaginable funds were attracted from the investors and finally met with a miserable death in 1949, ironically after prolonged imprisonment and humiliations.

Born as the son of a businessman Ponzi had a humble beginning as assistant teller in a bank owned by Zarossi, in Montreal. His experience with this bank helped him develop a new *modus operandi*, which later came to be known as Ponzi Schemes. The bank registered a phenomenal growth after it offered an interest of 6 per cent on deposits at a time when the rate offered by other banks was 3 per cent. Ponzi eventually became the manager of the bank.

He could observe that despite heavy burden of bad debt, Zarossi could meet the liability of interest payments using the money of new depositors and not through profit on investments. Like any other financial institution which offer unrealistic return, this bank also collapsed. Zarossi escaped to Mexico, taking away all the deposits of money.

Ponzi became jobless and after wandering in the streets in abject poverty, he approached a firm named Canadian Warehousing for a job. When he entered the office, there was no one and a *cheque book was found on the table. He forged the signature of the director and* wrote a cheque for $423.58 and encashed. He was arrested for the crime and spent three years in prison. He was released in 1911 and again got imprisoned for two years in another case.[2]

He left for US after releasing from prison. On landing at the Port he jotted down "I was five thousand miles away from home and five hundred or more miles away from my ultimate destination, in a strange country, with no friends and no money. My entire resource in cash was amounting to $2.50. I landed in this country with $2.50 in cash and $1 million in hopes, and those hopes never left me.[3]

He spent years doing odd jobs such as a dishwasher in a restaurant and did not mind sleeping on the floor. He lived in utter penury and to salvage himself he tried a hand in a number of businesses but failed in all.

Investment Scheme Based on International Postal Reply Coupon

Life was never the same for Ponzi when he received a letter from a company in Spain, where he worked earlier. The letter asked him about a catalog. There was an International Reply coupon inside. The purpose of the postal reply coupon was to allow him to pay the postage of a reply. He was seeing this for the first time.

He was astonished to see that the value of IRC is little higher in US and that he could exchange it for stamps of higher price than what is required to cover postage to Spain. He found a lucrative business opportunity in this venture as the cost of postage in Italy and Spain was very low than in US, after the First World War. It helped him to exchange it for U.S. stamps at a higher value, which could then be sold.

In his autobiography he recalls "Ponzi Finally Discovers An Untrodden Path to Fabulous Wealth and Takes It. The "racket" of international reply coupons actually fell in my lap like a ripe apple. I did not have to shake the tree to get it. I just reached over, where it had fallen, and took it. It looked good. Luscious. I examined it for flaws. Found none. I had to bite."

Ponzi claimed that buying stamps in Italy and selling them in another market at higher price brought him 400 per cent profit. This was not an illegal business. He resigned his stenographer's job and completely immersed in the new business.

Not satisfied with running the profitable scheme on his own, Ponzi began to seek investors in his business to turn even higher profits. Ponzi approached his friends offering 50 per cent dividend within 45 days, or 100 per cent return within 90 days. The amount collected was sent to relatives in Italy with instructions to buy and send back Postal Reply Coupons.

He kept the promise to the initial investors. He explained the payment was from the returns from postal reply coupons business. This incredible profit resulted in enthusiastic response from potential investor who flocked Ponzi's office. In reality, he was paying early investors using the money of later investors.

Ponzi satisfied the initial investors who asked for the Moon. He launched his own firm, the "Securities Exchange Company." People who tasted success were the best propaganda machinery. Agents were appointed for collecting the investments and they are paid exorbitant commissions on the collection.

By March 1920, his total collection was $30,000. Deposits started coming from far off states. Agents promoted the scheme aggressively and went for vigorous collection. By May 1920, he had made $420,000. People even mortgaged their houses for raising fund to deposit in Ponzi scheme, in anticipation of the heavy return. All the profits are reinvested. Ponzi called himself to be the eighth wonder of the world, the "Wizard" of finance who made $15,000,000 in nine months out of a six-cent coupon.[4]

He lived luxuriously. He splurged money for buying posh mansions and for charity. He opened accounts in various banks across the country. He donated $100,000 to the Children's Home in Jamaica in honour of his late mother.

He had deposit of 3 million in Hanover Trust Bank and using that bulk depositor capacity he influenced the bank and gradually became controller of the bank.

Robbing Peter to Pay Paul

Ponzi never cared the accumulating liabilities. Zarossi experiment of paying the existing investors using the fresh fund helped him to keep the balance for the time being. He did not design any legitimate business for generating income and profit. He was eventually landing up in heavy loss. "I was heading towards bankruptcy with the speed of a cannon ball. But I did not know it. Ignorance is bliss."

Ponzi sued for libel against a financial correspondent who wrote that there is no legal way of delivering such abnormal return and won $500,000 in damages. The onus of proof was on the writer as per defamation law, those days. Thus nobody dared to challenge the logic of his scheme. No probe was initiated.

He developed acquaintance with postal inspectors and police officers. Money sets its own rules. " At the height of my career, there were more inspectors working for me than for the city, and cops too. I had so many of them around that my office looked like police headquarters at roll call."

He managed to get an article published in Boston Post favouring his scheme. This again accelerated the flow. His daily collection went up to $250,000. Everyone, including politicians, law enforcement officers, and media persons were awed by the colossal stature Ponzi acquired within a short period of time.

"People wanted to know too much about my plans, more than was safe to tell. Had I been too liberal with information, somebody might have used it himself and left me out in the cold. So, I told just enough to whet the people's greed and curiosity. No more."

Even while all these were happening Ponzi's ship was slowly developing cracks. Unfazed by his stature some of the investigative financial reporters started probing the veracity of his claims. To make matters worse official probe was also initiated against. He played them all the tricks to delay an impending disaster.

Boston Post published a series of articles raising serious queries on the scheme. They observed that 160 million postal reply coupons would have to be in circulation if the total investment in Ponzi's scheme is to be covered. But, that much of reply coupons were never printed. Postal authorities came up with their statement challenging the claim of Ponzi. His castle of cards finally collapsed.

This stirred a hornet nest and caused a panic run on his office. But he is a person who believed was able to cope with any eventuality except death. For him life was one surprise after another. Some pleasant, some unpleasant, and he dealt with all these with a sense of humour.

He managed to contain the chaos made by the investors with a smile on his face. He served coffee and donuts to anxious investors who thronged his office. He paid out $2 million in three days to the suspicious investors. He was amused to see that majority of the investors was more than willing to put their money back to his kitty. Such was his power to rekindle the confidence. Within Forty-eight hours he was happy to see the million dollars coming back again in less time than it had taken to pay it out.

But the probing officers were compelled to check the records. They could see only index cards with investors' names. They struggled to assess the convoluted accounts to figure out the total volume of fraud and to track the fund. But they could never untangle it.

It was only much later it was established that Ponzi was merely 'robbing Peter to pay Paul'. In his autobiography Ponzi recalled: "People must have thought I had discovered the buried treasure of the Incas or Alladin's lamp. If they gave a thought at all to the coupons, they must have got dizzy figuring how many of them I needed to justify what I was doing. In fact, my visible resources then were in excess of $5,000,000. Assuming I earned two cents on each coupon, I should have had to handle over 250,000,000 of them! It was absurd. There were not that many in the world."

On August 2, 1920, Ponzi was declared hopelessly insolvent. His deposits were in Hanover Trust Bank. While Ponzi claimed $7 million in liquid funds, Audits revealed that Ponzi was at least $7 million in debt. Major withdrawals exhausted his reserves. It affected the entire banking system in the country.

Boston Post dug up his old stories of forgery conviction and his role at Zarossi's scandal-ridden bank. Banking Commissioner attached the properties of Hanover Trust Bank, where Ponzi had a key post.

Ponzi surrendered to federal authorities on August 12 and was detained for the charge of mail fraud. Five other banks in addition to Hanover Trust also suffered losses. His investors lost about $20 million in 1920.

He was charged in 86 mail fraud cases and was sentenced to lifetime imprisonment. Besides this he was charged for larceny. "Ponzi was back in court, facing trial on the first 10 larceny counts. Too broke to hire a lawyer, he served as his own advocate. Charismatic as ever, Ponzi was as persuasive in court as he had been among investors, and the jury found him innocent on all charges".[5] He came out pending appeal against all convictions but escaped to Florida.

Ponzi's Land Scheme

The irrepressible Ponzi launched another con scheme. He designed land based programme in the name Charpon Land Syndicate by September 1925. "The notorious crook went there to recoup the loss of his ill-gotten gains from his get rich quick scheme in Boston. He organised the Charpon Land Syndicate, which claimed it had an option on undeveloped tract of land near Jackson Ville (thought it was 65 miles away from there). He sought to obtain the capital required for the "purchase" by selling "unit certificate of indebtedness" at $ 310 per unit. He guaranteed a dividend of 200 per cent on each certificate within three months."[6]

But the land he sold to the depositors was underwater swampland in Columbia. He was treading into a new *modus operandi* which, after decades, has become the ultimate path of the con men the world-over for amassing billions.

Ponzi was again convicted for one year for violating the Florida trust and securities laws. Again he was freed after filing appeal. He was caught in the attempt to return to Italy disguising by shaving off his head and growing a moustache and was sent back to Massachusetts to finish his prison tenure.

After seven years of imprisonment he was released in 1934. There was an angry mob at the prison gate. He was deported to Italy. There also he experimented some schemes. He was not a person to be cowed down by adversities. Like a tragic hero he faced the inevitable fate with stoic resignation.

His last years were in poverty and sufferings. His eyesight failed and gradually became completely blind. He died in 1949 in a charity hospital in Brazil.

Business Model of Ponzi Scheme—As a Sly Game

A Ponzi scheme is a fraudulent investment scheme, whereby investors are paid from their own money or the money paid by subsequent investors, rather than from profit earned by the individual or organization running the operation. Offering of abnormally high returns is the tool used by such companies for persuading new investors to invest in the schemes. Attracted by the fabulous rate of return offered, more and more people will join the scheme investing money and such money is made use of to pay the initial members. An ever increasing flow of new investment is a pre-condition for keeping the scheme running uninterrupted.

Ponzi schemes are generally run by shell companies which do not manufacture anything or run any commercial services or which does not get any earning from other productive sources.

The income flow and viability of one Ponzi scheme based on some assumptions are depicted in the following schedule.

The model is based on the following assumptions:

1. A monthly return of 10 per cent is offered on the investment for a period of 36 months.
2. Only 1 individual is enrolled into the scheme every month.
3. All the members opt to deposit Rs. 10,000.

The first column of table 5.1 shows the growth of members in the scheme in every successive months. The second column shows the amount deposited by the new members.

The marginal revenue accruing to the company in every successive month, when an additional member enrolls the scheme making payment of Rs. 10,000 each, is shown in the third column. For example, in the first month though the member is depositing Rs. 10,000, after deducting the first month's 10 per cent return only Rs. 9,000 need be sent to the schemer. During the second month an amount of Rs. 2,000 is required for making pay out, i.e., Rs. 1000

Table 5.1

Cumulative total of members in the scheme	Amount deposited by the individual	Net Income accruing to the firm after paying 10% return to all members	Total net balance amount with the company	Liability of the company (10% return for 36 months)
1.	10,000	9000	9,000	35,000
2.	10,000	8000	17,000	69,000
3.	10,000	7000	24,000	102000
4.	10,000	6000	30,000	134000
5.	10,000	5000	35,000	165000
6.	10,000	4000	39,000	195000
7.	10,000	3000	42,000	224000
8.	10,000	2000	44,000	252000
9.	10,000	1000	45,000	279000
10.	10,000	0	45,000	305000
11.	10,000	–1000	44,000	330000
12.	10,000	–2000	42,000	354000.
13.	10,000	–3000	39,000	377000
14.	10,000	–4000	35,000	399000
15.	10,000	–5000	30,000	420000
16.	10,000	–6000	24,000	440000
17.	10,000	–7000	17,000	459000
18.	10,000	–8000	9,000	477000
19.	10,000	–9000	0	494000
20.	10,000	–10,000	–10,000	510000

each for the members who joined the scheme in the first and second month. After deducting Rs. 2000, only when the schemer borrows Rs. 10000, he gets only Rs. 8,000. Likewise in the third month, when he borrows additional 10,000, he gets only Rs. 7,000. Finally, in the 10th month he does not get anything even when an additional member deposits Rs. 10000 in his scheme. Subsequently, in 20th month the schemer's the net income becomes Rs. –10000.

The fourth column shows the gross income left with the company at the end of each month. The rate of growth of gross income shows a diminishing trend in each consecutive month. At the 10th level, the gross income stand still and in the subsequent months company's balance income falls despite receiving additional deposits of Rs. 10,000 each. At the end of 20th level the entire accumulated income with the company perishes to zero. Here the new deposits are not sufficient to meet the liability of 10 per cent return offer to all the members who were recruited into the scheme.

The last column shows the growth of liability of the company if it is to meet the promise. The company faces liquidity crunch and the accumulated liability grows at a faster rate.

If the schemer decides to stop the scheme and escape at the 10th level where his income is the maximum, 9 out of 10 of the total members loses different percentage of their deposited amount. If he fails to close the shutter at this optimum point his accumulated income falls and at the 20th level he becomes incapable of making pay as the amount reaches zero at this level. Even at this stage, 50 per cent of the member did not get back their deposited amount.

The real world situation is not comparable with this model. They accept huge investment and offer even more than 30 per cent return for 36 months.

The above model shows that the scheme is not viable even as a sly game as the company faces liquidity crisis at 20th level. The principle is to shut down the company and escape at the breakeven point where the balance income of the company is the maximum, i.e., 10th level in the given example. If the scheme is wound up at this level 90 per cent of the investors meet with loss. The question of honouring the offer is not at all the agenda in these sorts of schemes. The scheme offering 10 per cent monthly return cannot work after 20th level even as a game. It is not an investment policy and accumulated liability of the company will be piling at the end of each successive stage as shown in 5th column.

Modus Operandi of Ponzi Schemes

The following are the typical characteristics of a traditional Ponzi Scheme or a simple money circulation scheme.

The company or the person running the scheme will directly deal large number of depositors and will interact with all of them. The subscriber may not be required to enroll new members. The creamy layer in the society and dignitaries will be approached to invest in the schemes in the initial stage for attracting common people.

The schemes are enigmatic which offer higher returns than any legitimate business activity could plausibly sustain, and the investors are lured by offers. The greedy investors will soon create frenzy and will deposit all their life time earning. Investors may raise fund even by disposing their house or assets. They will soon find that their anticipation does not materialize and the offer of inflated rate of return is a deceptive tool of the scheme.

Imagination of the fraudsters and the gullibility of the investors may help in running the scheme for a short period. Ponzi schemes can survive simply by persuading most existing participants to reinvest their money. Often the high returns lead investors to leave their money in the scheme. Thus, the promoter do not have to pay out very much to investors. They simply have to send statements to investors showing them how much they earned.

The investors are persuaded to retain their return with the company itself by different methods. For minimizing withdrawals promoters offer new plans. Money is frozen for a longer period of time, in exchange for offer of higher returns. New cash flows are created by telling the investors that funds could not be transferred from the first plan to the second. Any requests of fund withdrawal will be allowed and promptly processed for creating an illusion to all other investors that the fund is solvent.

The companies go on advertising that they are engaged in the traditional business like trading in stock or bonds or dealing with Currency trading or real estate business. Thus, the schemes will be presented as a "Business Opportunity".

Inevitable Collapse

Once the requirements of new fund for meeting the commitments to the previous members exceed the actual new investments, the system is destined to collapse. The company becomes insolvent and will fall inevitably. The new offers will not be accepted by the public. Fund flow slows down and the promoter starts having problems paying the promised returns. A bank run like situation will be created soon as the investors create a panic asking for withdrawal of deposits. Such liquidity crisis leads to the ultimate collapse of the scheme.

Senior members will be benefited as payouts will be given in the initial stage as offered. The founders of the scheme and early members make huge gains while more than 90 per cent of the new members will lose their deposited money. The timing of enrollment decides whether a member becomes a beneficiary or victim.

The promoter vanishes with the remaining funds if the enforcement agencies could not stop the scheme at its early stage itself. A continual stream of investments by new members is inevitable for meeting the previous offers and to run the scheme.

Besides the model mentioned above, economic bubble comes in various forms. Ever rising prices of financial products like stock is an economic bubble created by market manipulation. Prices rise as the buyers bid more and the buyers do so as the prices are rising. Here also the prices exceeds the intrinsic value. But the cause for all economic bubble need not necessarily be the handiwork of single person who misrepresent the intrinsic value.

The Scottish Journalist Charles Mackay, who have written a history of the incidents which went to the extent of mass psychosis included Ponzi schemes and debunked this popular delusion.[7]

Ponzi scheme cannot continue after a given period and to overcome this, new pyramid schemes are devised by the con artistes which presuppose that the new investment in every month should be double that of the previous month, which will bring about sufficient fund to pay off the old depositors.

References

1. Charles Ponzi—*Digital History.*
2. http://en.wikipedia.org/wiki/Charles_Ponzi.
3. Ponzi, Charles (1936), *The Rise of Mr. Ponzi (Autobiography).*
4. *Ibid.*, Chapter VI.
5. Zuckoff, Mitchell (January 13, 2009), *"What Madoff could learn from Ponzi"*.
6. *The great American land bubble—A.M. Sakoloski,* page 341.
7. *Ponzi Schemes, Invaders from Mars, and More Extraordinary Popular Delusions and the Madness of Crowds,* by Joseph Bulgatz, (New York: Harmony Books, 1992), 11-45.

6
Pyramid Schemes

Mechanism for Avoiding Collapse

Simple Ponzi scheme cannot work beyond a particular stage unless more and more customers join the scheme. But, if the amount collected during one month is double that of the previous month, the amount will be sufficient to payoff the offered rate to all the senior members. This can be achieved easily by allowing each member in the scheme to enroll two more new investors into the scheme. Binary enrollment is devised as a tool for sustained growth of Ponzi Scheme.

The scheme will work out as a sly game by devising a tool for ensuring the expansion of the network of members in successive months in geometric progression, i.e. 2, 4, 8, 16, 32.... and so on. By the fairness of arithmetic the schemer will have a balance also after paying the entire upline members. The number of new investors at a particular layer of the pyramid will be greater than that of the total of all the previous members. It will be double that of the immediate previous stage.

The doubling of subscription in each consecutive period leads to the growth of investors in Pyramid model. In a pyramid scheme the new entrants create hierarchy by joining under the existing members. The number of members in the scheme increases at each successive layer in pyramid shape.

Genealogy or Binary Tree

Pyramid schemes are run by different companies with the help of computer, internet and software. There are websites for each company and the same can be accessed by entering user id and password of the members as authenticated from the server. It is customary in all the pyramid scheme software to show the spread of members under each member.

Every investor is placed at the top of a tree and he has to recruit new members into the scheme downline left and right. Genealogy shows the picture of binary tree of a subscribers, i.e., the spreading of the chain of customers under each investor. The following is the example of a binary tree.

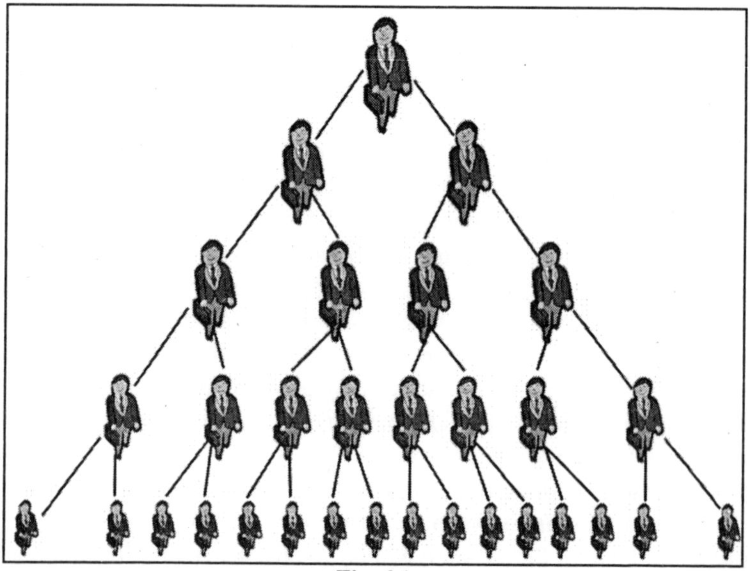

Fig. 6.1

Sponsoring a subscriber means referring a new customer directly to the scheme. Any member can sponsor any number of new subscribers but the enrollment will be under an existing member. Pyramid investment scheme will spread different areas at a very fast pace whereby an existing members in the scheme enrolled new members downline and the newly enrolled members again enroll fresh members and so on…Thus, the basic characteristic of this scheme is unlimited recruitment.

Thus, pyramid investment scheme also works by using the amount invested by the new members to make payments for the existing members. The scheme operates with the help of some tools for ensuring joining of new members in geometric progression.

The schemers never bother the growth of liability of the company at a rocket pace. Following the Ponzi legend, despite the accumulating liability the scheme can continue as a game without regard to the liability. The concern of the schemer is only to make the next month's payout and the question of clearing the total liability is not at all bothered.

Business Model of Simple Pyramid Scheme

A simple model of pyramid investment scheme can be built on the basis of the following assumptions:

Assumptions

1. An amount of 10 per cent of monthly return is offered to every member investing in the scheme, from the first month onwards, for a period of 36 months.
2. Though the real world companies are following most complicated scheme with multiple commission system. Here it is assumed that no other commission is offered to the members except monthly return named loyalty commission.
3. Every individual joins the scheme by remitting an amount of Rs. 10,000 to a company.
4. Each member enrolls two other members into the scheme under him in consecutive month.

Table 6.1

Level – month	*New member recruited during the month*	*Amount deposited by the new members in each successive months*	*Marginal Revenue accruing to the firm after paying 10% return to member*	*Total net balance amount with the company*
1.	1	10,000	9000	9000
2.	2	20,000	17000	26000
3.	4	40,000	33000	59000
4.	8	80,000	65000	124000
5.	16	160000	129000	253000
6.	32	320000	257000	510000
7.	64	640000	513000	1023000
8.	128	1280000	1026000	2049000
9.	256	2560000	2049000	4098000
10.	512	5120000	4097000	8195000

The first column shows the time circle, i.e. month. The second column shows the growth of the membership in the scheme at a geometric progression, as everybody enrolls two others, the new members enrolled in a given month will be double that of those enrolled in the previous month.

Third column shows the growth of deposits to the company.

The fourth column shows the additional income accruing to the company, when new members are enrolled, in each successive month, after meeting the payout liability at the rate of 10 per cent to all the members, i.e. during the second month, payout liability is Rs. 1000 to the member enrolled in the first month plus Rs. 1000 each to the members enrolled in the second month, i.e. Rs. 3000. After deducting Rs. 3000 from the income received during that month, net income accruing to the company is Rs. 20000–3000 = 17000.

The fifth column shows the total net balance amount available with the company after making all the payouts. For example, at the end of second month, total income with the company is Rs. 9000 collected during the first month plus Rs. 17,000 collected during the second month, i.e. Rs. 26,000.

The above schedule shows that schemer have sufficient money required for making payout. The total balance with the company grows heavily despite meeting all the payout liabilities.

Simple pyramid model investment scheme is devised by the con artistes to overcome the shortcoming of the conventional Ponzi scheme, i.e. the failure to ensure continuous flow of fund.

Thus, as a sly game the scheme can continue even after 20th or 30th level because the enrollments and corresponding new deposits doubles every month.

Here also working of the scheme is only as game and there is no intention of making payout to the downline members. Total liability of the company, if it is to meet the offer, is beyond imagination and there is no question of repayment to lower strata members. Large number of investors who join the scheme in the lower strata of the pyramid of investors will suffer undue loss without any return as they cannot find new gullible persons to enroll the scheme.

The compelling necessity of this scheme, if it is to work smoothly, is that the membership should grow at the geometric progression.

Unviability of Simple Pyramid Schemes

Perfect binary matching is arithmetically infeasible. Pyramid schemes always create pandemonium and investment frenzy as the greedy public will be motivated by the enormous offers. The scheme will spread virally from villages to villages and states to states. Thus, in the initial stage the network of investors will grow in geometric progression. The schemers accumulate billions in their accounts.

But as all the members of the society are not naïve sooner the downline members will start finding problems in making new enrollment. The network of investors will expand only few down layers and further expansion will become impossible. Then, only one leg will go down or will face a total halt.

As has been already pointed out the number of members required in the scheme. if there is perfect matching is calculated with the equation 2^{n-1}. By assigning value to n the number of members required at each successive levels can be calculated. After a few months it goes to alarming proportion.

The number of investors in the scheme at the end of 20th level is 524288. If it further goes down at the 30th level the number of members will be 120 crore, i.e. entire population of the country should become member. At the 32nd level the members required are $2^{31} = 2147483648$. The world population will be over at the end of 35th level.

After a few months of downward expansion the scheme will stand still. Down line members will find it difficult to enroll new members and thus binary matching will fail. This will lead to a sudden collapse of the scheme with millions of members at the lower level losing their whole deposit.

Business Model of Simple Pyramid Scheme When Binary Matching Fails

The simple pyramid scheme have the inherent flaw, which leads to its ultimate fall. In the absence of failure on the part of existing members to recruit new two members the scheme will collapse.

This is illustrated in the following schedule. The following schedule will show the cash flow when enrollment is assumed perfect up to 10th level.

Assumptions

1. The chain breaks after 11th level, i.e. one leg only is active.
2. After 15th level the downline members find it difficult to recruit new members and enrollment stops fully.
3. All investors deposit Rs. 10000 in the scheme.
4. Only Loyalty payment of 10 per cent is made to persons, from the first month onwards.

Table 6.2

Stage	*Newly enrolled members E*	*Total cumulative member*	*Deposit by the new members in each successive month—Column 1 × 10000*	*Commission liability Column No. 2 × 1000*	*Marginal Revenue accruing to the company after making payout*	*Total net balance available with the company*
1.	1	1	10,000	1000	9000	9000
2.	2	3	20,000	3000	17000	26000
3.	4	7	40,000	7000	33000	59000
4.	8	15	80,000	15000	65000	124000
5.	16	31	160000	31000	129000	253000
6.	32	63	320000	63000	257000	510000
7.	64	127	640000	127000	513000	1023000
8.	128	255	1280000	255000	1025000	2048000
9.	256	513	2560000	513000	2047000	4095000
10.	512	1025	5120000	1025000	4095000	8190000
11.	512	1537	5120000	1537000	3583000	11773000
12.	512	2049	5120000	2049000	3071000	14844000
13.	512	2561	5120000	2561000	2559000	17403000
14.	512	3071	5120000	3071000	2049000	19452000
15.	512	3585	5120000	3585000	1535000	20987000
16.	512	3585	0	3585000	–3585000	17402000
17.	512	3585	0	3585000	–3585000	13817000
18.	512	3585	0	3585000	–3585000	10232000
19.	512	3585	0	3585000	–3585000	6647000
20.	512	3585	0	3585000	–3585000	3062000
21.	512	3585	0	3585000	–3585000	–523000

The above schedule shows that the companies marginal income becomes minus at the 16th level. It takes only 4 months to deplete the accumulated income of the company if fresh enrollment fails totally. At the 21st level the company's total income will become negative.

The usual *modus operandi* is to close down the company at the breakeven point and the directors will abscond after sharing the balance income when the marginal income starts showing down trend.

The Scheme is only a false claim made to fraudulently induces persons to part with their money. The profitable working of the Scheme is impossible as no network can grow in geometric progression.

Pyramid Scheme with Multiple Commission Structure

Simple pyramid scheme fails when the new members fail to recruit others. The companies have experimented still newer model of pyramid schemes offering different types of incentives for ensuring the growth of enrollment in geometric progression.

The business model offered by the companies against whom crimes are registered the worldover shows that typically 3 types of commissions are offered in all these for ensuring the synchronized growth of the deposit. Subject to some minor variations, companies follow a standard *modus operandi* based three forms of return offer.

This is true in the Indian context also. The plan offered by most of the Indian companies like Tycoon Empire International, Visarave, Gold Quest etc. are all the schemes based on these three sorts of commission. The offers to lure the naïve and greedy public in such schemes include high monthly return, enrollment commission and inducement for making enrollment in binary pattern.

Loyalty Commission

The basic tool for luring the public for making investment in the pyramid scheme is offering very high monthly rate of return greater than any other regular investment opportunities. This is also known as Loyalty Commission. These are the income accruing to a member even when he does not enroll anybody under him. Loyalty commission is offered by different companies in different forms ranging from 1 per cent daily return for three years to 10 per cent monthly return for 36 months. This is the return offered in any Ponzi schemes whereas other offers are specific to pyramid scheme. The average rate of return in the economy is far below these offers and thus depositors will flock after the company.

Enrollment Commission

A commission will be offered in all pyramid schemes for inducing the members to recruit new investors into the scheme. This is known by different names like sponsor commission, spot commission, enrollment reward etc. Unlike Ponzi scheme where enrollment of new depositors is not expected from the investors, a pyramid scheme supposes every depositor to enroll new members into the scheme.

Though a member can enroll only two new recruits directly under him in the pyramid scheme based on binary plan, he can enroll more members under his downline members, and he will get the sponsorship commission for this.

For inducing this enrollment a minimum of ten percentage of the amount deposited by the new members are given to the sponsors as spot commission in all the pyramid schemes. New members can be enrolled only under an existing member. Members will go for aggressive enrollment chasing the offer of spot commission from the deposits of new investors.

Binary Matching Commission

Another form of commission offer is given for inducing the members to synchronize the growth of fund in each successive stage in geometric progression. This will be named binary matching commission or pair matching commission. Enrollment should be in a particular pattern ensuring at least that income collected from the new members in one month is double that of the previous month.

Not only the number of depositors but the deposited amount also should double in every successive layer.

Binary bonus is based on distributors downliner's enrollment. 10 per cent of the total invested amount, matched left and right will be issued to each subscriber as binary matching commission. The total amount earned by a member as binary matching commission depends not only on his personal enrollment but that of his downline members also. The companies give this commission on a monthly basis or fortnightly circle.

Binary matching commission is calculated in the following manner. Suppose billing cycle is one month, i.e. commission is calculated once in a month. Suppose member A is a top node and his total collection of deposit during one month is Rs. 100000 in the left side and Rs. 70000 on the right side. Here, amount matched left and right is only 70000. Binary matching commission, i.e., 10 per cent of the matched amount, i.e. 70000×10 per cent = 7000 will be paid.

Unmatched Point value is 100000–70000 = 30000. This unmatched PV will be carried forward to the next month. The unmatched amount will be considered for the next months calculation depending on that months business. Thus, only lower side is considered for binary matching commission and the remaining unmatched business volume is fleshed out to the next period.

In the initial days of the scheme all investors may be richly rewarded. Any such devious scheme of deception must initially catch the imagination of the gullible. With this end in view money will be pumped in at the initial stages to induce the gullible to enroll the scheme. Members are offered to become entitled to receive continuous flow of income which will be several multiples of the initial investment.

Business Model of Pyramid Scheme with Multiple Commission System

A study of nearly 30 companies which run pyramid schemes in India show that they used to collect money through the accounts in various banks, transfers the fund at the end of each month to another account and from there funds are again transferred in the individual accounts of large number of senior members in the scheme. These banks transfers itself proves that the schemes are only rotating money without making any value addition. There will not be much funds left over for making any investment in any productive field as the fund invested by the new members are used for making pay out to the senior members.

Thus, a generalized model can be set on the basis of some realistic assumptions, i.e. the plans followed by the companies are akin to the assumptions, except that actual rate of deposit in companies are lakhs.

Assumptions

1. The chain of investors goes on without break, i.e. every member recruits two more members every month.
2. Every member joins the scheme by depositing Rs. 10,000.

3. Members are paid a monthly return, Loyalty Commission, of 10 per cent of the investment.
4. Members are paid an enrollment commission of 10 per cent of the amount deposited by the new members enrolled by them, i.e. they get 20,000 rupees when they recruit two members into the scheme.
5. Binary matching commission is 10 per cent and there is perfect matching, i.e., amount deposited by the downline members in the left side matches perfectly with that in the right side of the tree.

Columnwise description of the Schedule (Table 6.3) is given below:

1. The billing cycle in the pyramid and MLM companies will be normally one month or fortnight. The level of advancement of the scheme in terms of this time cycle is shown in the first column.

2. The number of persons recruited in every successive month is shown in the second column. This shows a growth in geometric progression.

3. The total cumulative number of members in the scheme when it reaches successive levels is shown in the third column. The number of members in a particular level can be obtained by:

$$M = 2^{n-1}$$

where M = Total member in the scheme
n = Level time cycle the scheme has advanced.

At the 10th level the total number of members in the scheme would be:

$$2^{10-1} = 2^9$$
$$= 2\times2\times2\times2\times2\times2\times2\times2\times2 = 512.$$

4. The deposit made by the new members in each successive month is shown in the 4th column. As every member is assumed to join the scheme by depositing Rs. 10,000, the figure in the column is obtained by multiplying the figure in column No. 2 by 10,000.

Table 6.3

Level Month	Newly enrolled members E	Total cumulative member	Deposit by the new members in each successive month-Column 2 × 10000	Loyalty commission-Column No. 3 × 1000	Enrollment commission-Column No. 2 × 1000	Binary Matching Commission	Marginal Revenue accruing to the company after making payout-Column No. 4-(5+6+7)	Total net balance available with the company
1.	1	1	10,000	1000	0	0	9000	9000
2.	2	3	20,000	3000	2000	1000	14000	23000
3.	4	7	40,000	7000	4000	4000	25000	48000
4.	8	15	80,000	15000	8000	12000	45000	93000
5.	16	31	160000	31000	16000	32000	79000	172000
6.	32	63	320000	63000	32000	80000	217000	389000
7.	64	127	640000	127000	64000	192000	257000	646000
8.	128	255	1280000	255000	128000	448000	449000	1095000
9.	256	511	2560000	511000	256000	1024000	769000	1864000
10.	512	1023	5120000	1023000	512000	2304000	1281000	3145000
11.	1024	2047	10240000	2047000	1024000	5120000	2049000	5194000
12.	2048	4095	20480000	4095000	2048000	11264000	3073000	8267000
13.	4096	8191	40960000	8191000	4096000	24576000	4097000	12364000
14.	8192	16383	81920000	16383000	8192000	53248000	4097000	16461000
15.	16384	32767	163840000	32767000	16384000	114688000	10000	16471000
16.	32768	65535	327680000	65535000	32768000	245760000	16383000	88000
17.	65536	131071	655360000	131071000	65536000	524288000	65535000	65447000

5. The 5th column shows the total of loyalty commission to be paid by the company in the corresponding month. Monthly return of 10 per cent of the deposited amount has to be paid not only to the new recruits but to all the previous members also. Thus, the figure in this column is obtained by multiplying the total number of members in the scheme with the offered monthly return, i.e.:

$$2^{n-1} \text{ (R of D)}$$

where

"R" = percentage of monthly return offered, and
"D" = amount deposited by a member.

6. The liability of total enrollment commission to be paid by the company at different months is shown in the 6th column. During the first month there is only one member and thus no enrollment commission is paid. As 10 per cent of the deposited amount has to be paid to the sponsor, the figure in this column can be obtained by multiplying the number of new members in each time period with the monthly return amount to a single member.

7. The 7th column shows the amount to be spent by the company for paying the binary matching commission. When new members are enrolled into the scheme a large number of upline members are benefited out of this as it leads to matching of deposits by the group under them. In other words this is enrollment benefit.

A member who had enrolled in the scheme earlier is entitled to higher binary matching commission than a member who had joined in later stage.

The following schedule shows the binary matching commission of a person who is at the top of the binary tree, in the above mentioned plan with the given assumptions.

Table 6.4

Month/billing Cycle	*Number of members under the senior member*	*Amount matched left and right*	*Binary matching commission amount (10% of D)*
1.	0	0	0
2.	1 L and 1 R	10000	1000
3.	2 L and 2 R	20000	2000
4.	3 L and 3 R	30000	3000

During the second month one member is enrolled on the left and another on the right of the senior member. If everybody deposits 10000 the amount collected from the left downline is 10000 and that in the right downline also is the same. Thus, the matched amount is Rs. 10000 and the commission amount is its 10 per cent, i.e. Rs. 1000. Likewise, during the third month, the commission is Rs. 2000 and so on.

The number of members entitled to the binary matching commission goes on increasing in geometric progression, i.e. 1 member in the second month, 2 in the third, 4 fourth, 8 in the fifth month and so on.

The commitment of the company during a particular month is the sum of binary matching commission to be paid to the members at different layers.

Table 6.5: Schedule Showing Total Liability as Binary Matching Commission

Month/ Billing Cycle	*Number of new members enrolled*	*Total Number of members in the scheme*	*Commission to be paid to members joined at different layers*	*Total Binary matching commission liability to the company*
1.	1	1	0	0
2.	2	3	1x1000+ (2x0)	1000
3.	4	7	(2x1000)+(1x2000)+(4x0)	4000
4.	8	15	(4x1000)+(2x2000)+(1x4000)	12000
5.	16	31	(8x1000)+(4x2000)+(2x4000)+(1x8000)	32000
6.	32	63	(16x1000)+(8x2000)+(4x4000)+(2x8000)+(1x16000)	80000

During the first month as there is no enrollment binary matching commission is zero.

During the second month the first member enrolls two members left and right under him and thus he is entitled to a commission of Rs. 1000 as explained above. The two new members do not get any binary matching commission.

During the third month, the two members who joined the scheme during the second month enrolls two each under them and are entitled to get a commission of Rs.1000 each, i.e. 2×1000. At the same time by the third month the number of members under the member who joined in the scheme during the first month becomes 4 and thus he is entitled for a binary commission of 2000, i.e. 1×2000. The remaining four members who did not enroll anybody do not get any binary commission. Thus, the total liability of the company is $2 \times 1000 + 1 \times 2000 = 4000$.

At any stage the members who are enrolled in the scheme during that month is not entitled to any binary matching commission as he starts enrolling other on the next month onwards. The total number of men entitled to the Binary commission are those who joined the scheme in the *n*–1 level. The amount to be paid to a member is 10 per cent of half of invested amount as the commission is only for the amount matched left and right and not for the total deposited amount.

Thus, the total liability can be calculated as follows:

$$B = n-1\{E/2\ (r \text{ of } D)\}$$

Where:

B = The amount to be paid as binary matching commission.
n = The time cycle since the launching of scheme or else the level up to which the pyramid had grown downwards.
E = Newly enrolled members during that period.
r = % of deposits offered as binary matching commission.
D = Deposit made by an individual member.

For example total liability of the company during the 6th month is:

Total members by the 6th month = 63

Out of this, 32 have joined the scheme during 6th month and are not entitled to binary commission.

16 members enrolled during the 5th month have enrolled 2 members each and have collected 10000 from both. Thus, they are entitled to a commission of Rs. 1000 each. Company have to pay an amount of 16 × 1000 for the members enrolled in the 5th month.

Likewise 8 members who enrolled in the scheme during the 4th month is entitled to a commission of 2000 each, i.e. 8×2000.

4 members who enrolled in the scheme during the 3rd month is entitled to a commission of 4000 each and the total liability to them is 4×4000.

Two members who joined in the scheme is entitled to a commission of 8000 each during the 6th month and thus liability to them is 2×8000.

The one member who enrolled in the first month will get Rs. 16000 during the 6th month.

The total payout to be made by the company as binary matching commission is thus:

$$(16\times1000)+(8\times2000)+(4\times4000)+(2\times8000)+(1\times16000) = 80000$$

The simple way of calculating this using the equation is as follows:

$$\begin{aligned} B &= n-1\{E/2\ (r \text{ of } D)\} \\ B6 &= 6-1\{32/2\ (10\% \text{ of } 10000)\} \\ &= 5\ (16\times1000) \\ &= 80000. \end{aligned}$$

that is, during the 6th month the company will have to spend Rs. 80000 towards the binary matching commission.

Unviability of the Scheme even as a Sly Game

The percentage of Marginal Revenue to be set aside for making payout in each successive month shows an increasing trend in the given business model.

The above schedule shows that 30 per cent of the income accruing to the company is to be set aside during the second month for making payout the existing members, i.e. the income received by the company as deposit by the company enrolled into the scheme during that month is Rs. 20000. The commitment of all the payouts, i.e. the sum of loyalty commission, enrollment commission and binary matching commission together is Rs. 6000. Thus, the percentage of additional revenue to be set aside for making pay is only 30 per cent, i.e. Rs. 6000 is 30 per cent of Rs. 20000.

As the company goes on recruiting more members in each successive month, it can be seen that the percentage of additional income accruing to the company to be set aside for making payout shows an increasing trend. The following schedule will explain this.

Table 6.6

Month/Billing Cycle	*Marginal Revenue during the given stage*	*Total payout liability (loyalty +enrollment+ Binary Commissions)*	*Total payout liability as a % of marginal revenue*
1.			
2.	20000	6000	30%
3.	40000	15000	37.5%
4.	80000	35000	43.75%
5.	160000	79000	49.4%
6.	320000	175000	54.68%
7.	640000	383000	59.84%
8.	1280000	831000	64.92%
9.	2560000	1791000	69.96%
10.	5120000	3841000	75.01%

During the second month only 30 per cent of the marginal income is spent for making payout. But at the 10th level it is seen that 75 per cent of the additional income is to be spent for making payout during that month. The above schedule shows that the percentage of income to be set aside for meeting the committed liability is showing an increasing trend and the rate of growth is nearly 5 per cent. It would mean that at the 15th level 100 per cent of the income collected by the company from the new members.

The above business model shows that in the initial stages, despite making loyalty commission, spot commission and very high binary matching commission, the company is still left with sufficiently huge amounts. The amount piling in the company running this con game is shown in the column No. 8. The exorbitant payout to the initial members in the form of these commissions leads to good enrollment in the initial period.

But the rate of growth of company's income declines at a steady rate and the marginal income becomes negative at 16th level. Thus, the total income also shows a declining trend at this level. The very next level, it is seen that the total income also becomes negative, meaning thereby that the company is not in a position to meet the promise even by using the accumulated income during the previous months.

Thus, the scheme have a breakeven point, i.e. the point at which the marginal income becomes zero and total income is the maximum. The shrewd con artiste will shut down the company at this stage and will abscond with the enormous amount.

Thus, the directors of the company running this model of business always take precautions to hide his identity for evading tracking by the investing officers when the scheme collapses. The company will be registered in fake address; the directors on record will be the proxy of the actual ones. Even the bank account will be the one opened in bogus address.

Deceptive Tools for Trimming Down the Payments

The companies will meet with a fast collapse if commissions are paid at the above rate. Thus, instead of actually making the payment of commissions, the con artistes further devised tools which help in creating an impression the commissions are earned. Gullible can be easily duped and actual money payments are not required. These tools are used for trimming down the payouts. This includes re-investment persuasion, E-wallet, offering of new schemes and re-pyramiding etc.

Re-investment

In their pursuit for easy money the senior members in the scheme will go for aggressive enrollment and besides friends and relative they will fill make self-enrollment. The scheme works as no substantial payout is not required as the greedy members will enroll themselves in the downline again and again reinvesting the receipts from the company. This will reduce the payout liability of the companies.

E-Wallet

This is a typical cheating tool in all the pyramid investment schemes. Electronic Wallet is designed for shifting the unpaid earning of the depositors and this is presented as upcoming payout amount. Payout will be made only on specific demand from the members. The company will defraud the depositors by showing some amount in the E-Wallet without making actual payment.

Offering New Schemes and Re-pyramiding

When the schemes are about to collapse for want of new members, the existing members themselves may be induced to make investment by offering new schemes basis.

These gimmicks are not sufficient to stop the ultimate fall of the company due to inherent flaws and the fraudsters will take away the huge accumulated fund at the breakeven point.

Percentage of Members Losing in the Scheme

The pyramid investment schemes are extremely harmful as the proportion of members losing their money in the scheme is alarmingly high. In a binary scheme, if only loyalty commission is considered, for getting back the principal amount only, 9 months are required. Thus, regardless of the stage at which the scheme collapses, members in bottom 9 levels always lose their money. Also the customers who do not go for aggressive enrollment will face this fate.

Suppose the company offers 10 per cent return on a given month. Thus, to get back the principal amount it takes 10 months. At whatever level the scheme collapses, the entire members who joined the scheme during that month will lose 100 per cent of the deposited amount. The number of members who joined the scheme in the last month will be double that of previous month. Those who joined the scheme one month prior to the collapse might have received only one month's return and loses 90 per cent of the invested amount. Those who joined the scheme 2 months prior to the fall might receive 20 per cent and loses 80 per cent of the deposit and so on.

Viability of such scheme as a game can be judged on the basis of the proportion of members who loss in the scheme as percentage of the total members in the scheme. This can be calculated as follows:[1]

The total members in the scheme at any point can be calculated by 2^n, where n stands for the number of layers which the particular scheme has reached.

Pyramid schemes spread from the top. When each member enrolls two new members each, at *n*th level down from the top, there are 2^{n-1} members.

At n-1 level, down from the top there are 2^{n-2} members
At n-2 level, down from the top there are 2^{n-3} members etc.
At n-8 level down, there are 2^{n-9} members

The total of members in all these 9 levels together is:

Total members = 2^{n-1}
Percentage of members losing money =
Total members in the last nine stages/Total members.

$$= (2^{n-1} + 2^{n-2} + 2^{n-3} + 2^{n-4} + 2^{n-5} + 2^{n-6} + 2^{n-7} + 2^{n-8} + 2^{n-9})/2^n-1$$
$$> 511/512 = 99.8 \text{ per cent (approximately)}$$

Considering the enrollment commission and binary matching commission also, even assuming that a minimum downward expansion of 3 layers is required for recouping the principal amount, proportion will be:

$$\text{Members Losing Money} = 2^n + 2^{n-1} + 2^{n-2}$$
$$\text{Total Members} = 2^{n+1}-1$$

If we neglect the quantity of 1 subtracted in the denominator, we get the inequality;

$$\text{Members Losing Money} > 2^n + 2^{n-1} + 2^{n-2}$$
$$= 2^{n-2}(2^2 + 2 + 1) = 2^2 + 2 = 1 = 7$$
$$\text{Total Members} = 2^{n+1}-1$$
$$= 2^{n-2} \quad (2^3)$$
$$= 2^3 \quad = 8$$
$$\frac{\text{Members Losing Money}}{\text{Total Members}} > \frac{7}{8} = 87.5\%$$

Thus, the proportion of members losing by making investment in a binary model pyramid scheme, regardless of the stage at which the scheme collapses, will be around 87.5 per cent or more. Still the requirement of recruitment of only 2 by each members, i.e. expansion in geometric progression act as an invisible psychological pull luring the people into this fraud game.

Pyramid schemes works by defrauding the members at the bottom by those on top. "It's a mathematical fact that no matter how many people join a pyramid scheme, 88 per cent of the members will be on the bottom level and will lose their money."[2] Pyramid schemes are illegal because people don't lose their money due to normal market forces but because the system requires them to lose so that a few at the top will win.

While joining everybody imagine himself to be at the top of the pyramid. But when he fails to find new members to recruit and thereby build his downline, he will realize that he is actually at the bottom. The natural plight of large number of investors at the bottom is to face the loss when the scheme collapses. The very structure of this matrix shows that whenever the collapse occurs, at least 80 per cent will be in the bottom level with no means to make a profit. Even those people one level above the bottom will not have recouped their investment.

In some other alternative schemes such as Matrix plan etc. each member is supposed to enroll 3 each. Such schemes will spread more virally and will meet with sudden collapse.

Such schemes are extremely dangerous from Society's point of view because to gullible public, the scheme looks very attractive, the opportunity of being self-employed and earning money sitting at home by contacting family and friends appeal to most of the people.

The initial pyramid scheme appeared in the form of chain letters. The "send-a-dime" letter appeared in Denver in 1935, bearing the heading "Prosperity Club" and the slogan "In God We Trust". You will be sent a list of participants and will be required to send a dollar to the person at the top of the list. At the same time you can add your name at the bottom of the list. You can then mail copies of the letter to your contacts with instructions to do the same. A large variety of this chain letters are there in the Internet.

It is no more a silly game but assumes the dimension of an organized crime with the proceeds extending beyond billion. It comes in various forms disguised as games, motivational courses, buying clubs, mail order operations, chain letters, or multilevel marketing businesses. There are countless variations of the pyramid investment scheme, spread in every nook and corner of the world, which goes unregulated.

Mathematical unviability as a game, infeasibility as an investment scheme, and the immense potential for the criminals organizing such schemes for grabbing the income of the masses lead the legislators to outlaw such scheme in all the countries.

Wherever a new scheme is launched, gullible and naïve public, create a pandemonium and investment frenzy seeing the return flow pumped out to the initial investors. People risk their money and once the scheme collapses, they lose their reputation and relationships also. When the scheme collapses the recruits at the bottom have no option other that turning to their higher ups. Frustration, disappointment, confusion and loss are the ultimate aftermath of these to majority of the members.

References

1. Michael Sakowski, *Mathematics of Pyramid Scheme: The Scam Explained.*
2. Fitz Patrick, MLM Truth.

7
Multi-Level Marketing

After realizing the inherent dangers of Ponzi and Pyramid Schemes, many countries have come down heavily on the companies running these schemes. But those who indulge in the business are smarter and are known for their proclivity to stay afloat even in the difficult environment. This survival instinct has led the formation of a new scheme named Multi-Level Marketing (MLM), which is nothing but wolf in sheep's clothing.

MLM as Camouflaged Pyramid Scheme

Pyramid and Ponzi schemes are destined to collapse as it faces liquidity crunch when the flow of new money stops as the network fails to expand. The network cannot spread further once the saturation point is reached. Then they fail to keep the promises and the scheme collapses.

But, if the companies cleanly state that you can earn a return only if you enroll more and more members, there is no question of such immediate collapse. In the Pyramid schemes, Loyalty commission is the return offer made to members even if he does not enroll anybody. MLM scheme does not offer any loyalty commission, i.e., a member is entitled to commission only if he enrolls. In most of the MLM schemes there are only enrollment commission and pair matching commission.

Unlike Pyramid scheme, the MLM will sustain for long as the offer is to pay commissions only to those who enroll further members. Members who cannot bring more members into the scheme cannot complain and instead are bound to accept their failure.

Everybody joining the scheme by purchasing a product have to enroll others by selling these products to them. The working mechanism is the same as that of the pyramid scheme except that the collection of deposit is in the form of price of a product. Overtly product is only a cover to run the pyramid scheme.

Instead of collecting deposit from members by offering fabulous return, here the company collect this in the form of price of a product sold to them. Besides the actual price, the deposit to the pyramid scheme also will be hidden in the price of the product. Here "enrollment" becomes "sales" and return on investment becomes commission on product sales. MLM companies compel the members to sell the products and to build a downline, offering heavy commissions.

Several studies show that the price of the products sold by the MLM companies is invariably several multiples of its actual market price. A look on the price list of products sold by the MLM companies in India shows that, the products are priced 8 to 13 per cent higher than its actual market price. The price list of the products sold by Amway, RMP etc. testifies this.

Thus exorbitant prices coupled with enrollment of further sellers by every purchasers of the product together constitute the basic requirement of Multi-Level Marketing.

The products, no units of which can be sold in the open market, can be sold rampantly if it is supported by pyramid model enrollment. Members join the scheme chasing the mirage of exaggerated income opportunity and the flamboyant life style of the senior members. Most of them spend more than what they earn.

It is a simple fact that no MLM scheme can be run if the products are sold at its actual market price. Hiding of pyramid scheme under the garb of product sale can be done in several ways.

MLM Based on Cheating Products

One way hiding pyramid scheme behind product sale is to develop some worthless products which have only trivial cost or value and collecting money using the product as a token. Companies design some totally worthless products which are not commonly available in the market and are sold at astronomical price. The members in the network purchase and sell these products knowing well that the products only have an assumed value.

These worthless products purchased by the gullible as they anticipate fabulous commission when they "distribute" the same to the downline members. Thus, the products that question the very sanity of a person becomes the focal point of the business. Gradually, even the token would disappear and the business will become pure and simple pyramid scheme. The sale is only for recording the deposit.

The absurdity of the business would become evident if one examines the products that are circulated as part of these schemes aided by ample doze of propaganda. Thus, a bracelet made of imitation gold worth Rs. 10 can appear as 'nano bracelet' that would cost Rs. 10,000. The propagators of these products will quote from some obscure text to "prove" it would increase blood circulation and is the panacea for all the illness. Another hilarious example is the Tobacco card. This plastic card is sold among smokers who are anxious to get rid of its ill effects. If you have an alcohol card in your pocket, you can drink to glory and yet are protected from the hazards of drinking!

Those who join the scheme willingly suspend their disbelief and draw others to the make belief world.

MLM based on Quality Products

Another method is to sell the product at 10 times higher than the actual market price. Pyramid model money circulation scheme can be run; camouflaged behind the sale of standard products also. Company can collect Rs. 10000 from a member by selling a product worth Rs. 1000 at Rs. 11000 or by selling a worthless product without any cost at Rs. 10000.

Surpassing the small players in the market, the transnational conglomerates have invented a more "rational" way to run the con game. For avoiding allegations of cheating the people by selling worthless product, they select quality products. But the price of the product sold by the MLM companies will be several multiples of their actual market prices. People are ready to pay the exorbitant price as the companies offer unimaginable commission when they enroll downline members.

Most of these companies do not manufacture anything and instead outsource the products from other manufacturers. Most of the MLM products are out sourced and the companies do not engage in manufacturing on their own. The same products are sold in the market at much lower price by the manufacturing companies in another brand name.

Entry Kit

Yet another way of hiding the investment to pyramid scheme is to collect money from the members as entrance fee. It is customary in the MLM schemes that the new entrants have to pay a fee for playing the game. This is collected in different forms. Some of the firms make it mandatory for the new members to purchase the pamphlets, CDs and other marketing tools which explain how to lure the others into the scheme.

If new recruits have to pay an entry fee of Rs. 5000, only the remaining amount need be hidden in the price of the product.

MLM Business Model

MLM or Product Selling Pyramid is the most cruel and deceptive of all the fraudulent schemes as approximately 99 per cent of the participants are destined to experience loss and disappointment. This was established beyond doubt by researchers like John M. Taylor and Fritz Patric who undertook painstaking studies of more than 500 MLM companies.

For explaining a Multi-Level Marketing Model we make the following assumptions:

1. There is one single product and a member can join the scheme by purchasing that product.
2. Everybody joining the scheme will have to enroll two members by selling two units of the product.
3. Every unit of the product is sold at a price of Rs. 6000.
4. The purchase cost of the product is Rs. 1000, i.e. there is a net margin of Rs. 5000 to the company in one unit sale.
5. There is an entry fee of Rs. 5000 for every member.

6. 10 per cent of the net margin is offered as direct sales commission.
7. 10 per cent of the net margin on every sale is offered as binary matching commission.
8. There is perfect binary matching, i.e. every member makes two sales during a month.

Table 7.1

Time cycle	*New sales*	*Total entry fee remitted by the new members*	*Total margin on sales earned by the company*	*Total marginal income-3+4*	*Direct sales commission*	*Total Binary matching commission*	*Net Revenue after paying commission*
1.	1	5000	5000	10000	—	—	10000
2.	2	10000	10000	20000	2000	1000	17000
3.	4	20000	20000	40000	4000	4000	32000
4.	8	40000	40000	80000	8000	12000	60000
5.	16	80000	80000	160000	16000	32000	112000
6.	32	160000	160000	320000	32000	80000	208000
7.	64	320000	320000	640000	64000	192000	384000
8.	128	640000	640000	1280000	128000	448000	704000
9.	256	1280000	1280000	2560000	256000	1024000	1280000
10.	512	2560000	2560000	5120000	512000	2304000	2304000

The first column in the above schedule shows the time period since beginning and the second column shows the growth of members into the scheme.

The third column shows the total amount earned by the company as entry fee remitted by the new members, i.e. this is obtained by E×D, where E is the number of new entrants during a particular month and D is the Entry Fee to be paid by a member. During the second month 2 members are joining the scheme and thus total entry fee is 2 × 5000 = 10000.

Fourth column shows the net total gain on the sale of product, i.e. the sum of sales margin over the purchase price of products during a particular month. As purchase price of the product is only Rs. 1000, the margin per unit of sale is Rs. 5000 and the total of such margin is thus E × P, where is the number of new entrants which is equal to the sale during that month and P, the margin per unit.

Fifth column shows the total additional income earned by the company during each successive month, which is the sum of all entry fee and margin on unit sales, i.e. the sum of entries in column Nos. 3 and 4. This column shows that the income accruing to the company is the same as that of running a pure pyramid scheme where the investment by a single person is Rs. 10000. Here the investment is hidden in the price of the product and in entry fee partially. The only difference is that sale of one product also goes on.

Sixth column shows the liability of the company for meeting the direct sales commission. Thus, when one member is enrolled by purchasing a unit of the product, the company gets Rs. 5000 as entry fee and another 5000 as margin on price, i.e. sales price Rs. 6000- purchase price Rs. 1000. Thus, total net earnings to the company when a unit of the product is sold is Rs. 10000. 10 per cent commission would mean that for each enrollment or sale company have to spent Rs. 1000. This is nothing but the direct sponsorship commission in the pyramid scheme.

Seventh column shows the liability of the company for making payout of binary matching commission during each successive month. A member is entitled to get binary matching commission when he makes two sales to the downline members. The calculation is done in the same manner as in pyramid model and the figures are the same.

$$B = n-1\{E/2\ (r \text{ of } D)\}$$

where n is the time cycle since beginning of the scheme, E is the total number of members in the scheme, r is the rate of binary matching offered and D is the total net margin accruing to the company when one sale is made.

$$\begin{aligned} B6 &= 6 - 1\{32/2\ (10\% \text{ of } 10000)\} \\ &= 5\ (16 \times 1000) \\ &= 80000, \end{aligned}$$

i.e. during the sixth month the company will have to spend Rs. 80000 towards the binary matching commission.

The last column shows the total net margin accruing to the company in each successive month after meeting all the payout liabilities. This column shows that the company's income is almost doubling every month. The total accumulated income also grows at a very fast rate.

From the total income only direct sales commission and binary matching commission liability is to be deducted. No loyalty bonus or regular income offer is made here. Thus, nobody will claim any income from the company if he cannot make any additional enrollment or sale. It would otherwise mean that members will be ready to accept their failures. The millions who join the MLM scheme in the lower strata will have to go without any return or else they are destined to purchase the product at several multiples of its actual market price.

The proportion of people losing in the scheme would be almost 99 per cent and this was explained by Fritz Patric. Thus, product selling pyramid scheme or MLM is the most cruel and exploitative of all the money circulation scheme. I offer a safe conduit for the companies for robbing the income of the income of the consumers who buy the product.

Still corporate lobbying and manipulative tactics are well under way round the world to depict MLM as direct selling and to legalize the system.

Some of the companies claim that they do not charge any entry fee. The price of product sold by such companies would be ten times or more than its actual market price. Imagine that an MLM company purchases a product worth Rs. 1000 from the manufacturer. This product is sold to the members of the scheme at 11 fold price, i.e. Rs. 11000. Individual A can join the scheme by purchasing a Product. The remittance to the company minus the product price can be deemed to be the deposit in money chain.

. Thus, when a new member enrolls the scheme by purchasing a product, he makes an actual deposit of Rs. 10000. He has to sell the product to two members, i.e., 'B' and 'C', at the same rate and can enroll them as downline members under individual 'A'. When he makes two sales of the product, together their deposit to the company is Rs. 20000, when members B and C both makes two sales each. Thus at the 3rd level total sale is 4 units and the total deposit made by the new members to the company is Rs. 40000. In this way the enrollment of members and company's income double at every successive layers down from the top. Thus, it is not necessary that entry fee is an integral part of all MLM.

This is nothing but pyramid scheme except that sale of some products also takes place along with enrollment to money circulation scheme. Thus, the basic characteristics of an MLM are selling of product at exorbitant prices through a network of members which expands when existing members enroll new members. In other words irrational pricing and stipulation to the purchasers that they should become sellers are the hallmark of an MLM scheme.

Depending on the nature of enrollment pattern, a large variety of puzzling schemes are available in the public domain. For avoiding the word pyramid, the expansion of the network can be altered to several other patterns by letting every member to enroll more members instead of two. Also blending of entry fee or re entry fee with irrational price is done in complex ways by the con artistes and this will be analysed in the ensuing chapters.

MLM as an Unethical Marketing Plan

Authors who have studied the operations of MLM companies in depth, like John M. Taylor and Fritz Patric have concluded that MLM is nothing but an unethical marketing plan based on deception.

1. *The most unfair part of MLM is that it gives opportunity to a chosen few to earn huge income while majority of downline members are destined to be the losers. The senior members get a fat purse without sweating their eyebrows.*
2. *It is a money transfer scheme, that lead to unjust enrichment of a few at the* top level disproportionate to their efforts while large mass of people fall prey to this.
3. Millions of consumers are enticed to buy worthless products or *purchase products at a price much higher than the market price.*
4. MLM companies normally sell "pills, potions, and lotions" or other products that are unique so that their quality cannot be compared with similar like products available in the market.[1]
5. *MLMs are spread like contagious decease and* attack the most vulnerable sections in the society cutting across geographical boarders.
6. *A robust economy cannot allow unfair practice like MLM as it will drain the capital and funds from legitimate businesses.*

As these companies are non productive its emergence for counterproductive for other business opportunities.

7. *Loss rates are extremely high.* Spending more on company purchases than they receive in commissions from the company is the most objectionable harm.
8. *MLM companies survive by deception and Misrepresentations. Thus the income generated from such schemes are* "theft by deception," and certainly ill-gotten gain.
9. Infinite markets based on endless entrepreneurial chains, does not exists in the real world and thus they are destined to perish and face market saturation and collapse. Expanding to virgin markets and new countries and re-pyramiding in the same markets with new product are the techniques to avoid instant dooming.
10. *Recruiting MLMs evolve into Ponzi schemes. Later entrants find it difficult to move on in the recruiting effort. The company which cannot take initiative for re-pyramiding at this stage normally close down and escapes.* Introducing new products, entering new geographic regions are real challenge and in its absence, the members will lose their income stream and the position they gained and the company may collapse.
11. *Stockpiling of products is common*, a fact seldom admitted by MLM participants. Many wind up making excessive purchases in their own name or in the name of downline "distributors" in order to advance up the hierarchy of participants.
12. MLM is an aggravated version of the no product pyramid scheme as it is bound to have a higher rate of loss and affect far more victims. The ending scene of the drama will be products not sold, promises not kept and dreams not realized. Robert Fitz Patrick shows that more than 99 per cent of all MLM participants lose money every year. "Yes, 99 per cent. That is not hyperbole. The data offered by the MLM companies themselves confirm this amazing fact. MLM, therefore, cannot be called a "business opportunity". The idea of MLM offering the average person a viable or

an "extraordinary" income is a myth, which is to say, a *lie*."[2]

13. The high prices at which the products are sold are not set by the legally permissible "brand loyalty" based on quality, or by the market mechanism of demand and supply but by the illegal system of participation payment and enrollment payment.

Value System and Social Implications

MLM inculcates a new value system in the society, carnivalizing the greed and craze, and breeding endless infatuations for gain. Robert Fitz Patrick writes: "The commercialization of family and friendship and the use of "warm leads" advocated in MLM marketing programmes are a destructive element in the community and very unhealthy for individuals involved. People do not appreciate being pressured by friends and relatives to buy products."[3]

Tainted personality and blemished social foundation will be the ultimate outcome awaiting the MLM junkies as their business is built by capitalizing and exploiting the personal relations. Gradually, they develop it to be a life style, get addicted to MLM and faces problem while working in other business with normal settings. Silently they will realize that they are used as dupe to swindle their friends and relatives.

Scheibelers is right in asserting that it is merchandising on deception "Already, I have lost almost every friend I ever had, been bankrupted.... It is a strange irony that those I loved the most, now see me as the enemy. Many of my closest friends have participated effectively in our character assassination. Some pray for us, believing that Satan is using us to do a great evil."[4]

The techniques of Cult Mind Controls, which were used in religious congregations, are now being used in the business meets for mentally conditioning the sales man and consumers, preventing critical judgments. They have proved that even the educated and intelligent consumers can be seduced through the indoctrination camps preaching the virtues of MLM. Networking groups are often referred to as "Communion", with spiritual connotations. Here wealth is made the centre of all the prayers, hope and dreams.

Confused Enforcement

There is an all-round chaos in the matter of enforcement of laws against this open robbery and as has been mentioned by John Taylor law enforcement is confused everywhere.

When legal steps are initiated the companies come up with the claim that what they run is not pyramid scheme and they are engaged only in the sale of products. Political parties goes to their support in the name of direct selling associations to protect them from the strangle hold of law.

When the enforcement agencies pound on the companies, they attempt to manipulate public opinion to their favour through some standard methods. They successfully get some "guidelines" issued by the governments in the name of "controlling and restraining" the companies. But rather than controlling these guidelines will have provisions which will give an impression that if these guidelines are followed the scheme becomes legal.

The guidelines issued in various countries and various states are the same though these are claimed to be the product of expert committee recommendations. These are the brain product of Multi National fraudulent firms.

None of the guidelines ever restrict the two inherent attributes of MLM, i.e. exorbitant price and endless chain of distributors. The directives will insist the companies to follow some innocuous conditions such as companies should have their website with full address of the members, buyback offers for the products etc.

Though the guidelines are issued ostensibly to protect the rights of the consumers, they become a tool for the companies to attain a sense of legality for the schemes that exploit the consumers. This does not impose any control on MLM.

Strangely none of these guidelines defines what MLM is. Strangely some of the Indian states have enacted new laws conveniently defining direct selling and MLM as if both are synonymous. All these call for the need for a new approach to define Multi-Level Marketing from the enforcement angle.

References

1. John, M. Taylor, *The Network Marketing Game: Gospel Perspectives in Network Marketing.*
2. Robert Fitz Patrick—Report on the commission payouts of 11 major MLMs.
3. *False Profits*, by Robert Fitz Patrick. (Herald Press: Charlotte, N.C., 1997).
4. *Merchants of Deception*—Scheibeler.

8
Definition of MLM from Enforcement Angle

The absence of a clear cut definition of MLM in law is the major hurdle for the effective enforcement of punitive measures. Thus, a simple and transparent definition of the concept of MLM is a prerequisite in the legal battle against these companies.

There has been no dearth of definition of MLM in the academic realm with different authors coming up with interpretations of their own. Each one emphasis on a particular attributes of the concept but none of them covers all the basic traits of the concept. The pen pushers for the Multinational companies have succeeded in smuggling in the idea that there exists some "Real MLM" that are engaged in genuine business. The division between real and fraudulent MLM is only imaginary to hoodwink the legislators and investigators. When the very business model of MLM is proved to be illegal and deceptive, what is the logic behind such segregation?

Richard Poe defines Network Marketing as "Any method of marketing that allows independent sales representatives to recruit other sales representatives and to draw commissions from the sales of those recruits.[1]

This definition is not comprehensive as it does not mention the abnormal price level which is not determined by demand or supply forces. Also, the endless chain of sales persons growing in pyramid model leading to market saturation is not given due to thrust in this approach.

Yet another definition of the MLM is the one given by Zig Zigler: "Network marketing is a system for distributing goods and services through networks of thousands of independent sales people, or distributors. The distributors earn money by selling goods and services and also by recruiting and sponsoring other salespeople who become part of their downline, or sales organization. Distributors earn monthly commissions or bonuses on the sales revenues generated by their downline".[2]

It is an abortive attempt to defend the MLM by presenting a distorted version of the occult schemes and claims it to be legal and ethical and does not mention the easy money offer and endless chain characters of the scheme.

The US Federal Trade Commission have quoted the definition of MLM given by P.J. Vander and William Keep, in its Revised Proposed Business Opportunity Rule: "Multi-level marketing is one form of direct selling, and refers to a business model in which a company distributes products through a network of distributors who earn income from their own retail sales of the product and from retail sales made by the distributors' direct and indirect recruits. Because they earn a commission from the sales, their recruits make, each member in the MLM network has an incentive to continue recruiting additional sales representatives into their downlines."[3]

This definition has been the selling point of fraudulent companies the world over as it cleverly manipulates the illegal schemes into a legally acceptable merchandise activity. This enable the companies to float their own trade union under the banner of direct selling demanding to differentiate direct selling from Pyramid Schemes. This is overtly absurd.

The logic of objecting pyramid scheme is not because of its shape but the arithmetic infeasibility of the scheme. Pyramid expands only in one direction. In the name of differentiating direct selling from pyramid, FTC advocates for the more precarious sun flower schemes, which grows in all direction. This is the scheme followed by the US based companies like Amway, Herba Life, Tupper Ware etc.

This is highly misleading and unacceptable as it is designed with the ulterior motive of defending the American Conglomerates in perpetuating their economic invasion of the world and to augment the economic drain from the Third World. The system which allows indefinite number of intermediaries, who are paid from the price of the product, are claimed to be direct selling.

FTC had initially set forth a rule that MLM companies should make at least 70 per cent of the sales to the purchasers outside the pyramid at the market price, i.e. they need not join the scheme for buying the product. This reasonable norm was later on diluted.

MLM is repeatedly proved to be a system, whose working mechanism will fail if the products are offered at the price set by market forces.

The unholy nexus between FTC and MLM industry is brought forth by John Tailor who alleged that FTC has given up its mission to protect consumers against unfair and deceptive practices.

Tailor defined Multi-Level Marketing (MLM) as "a purported income opportunity, in which persons recruited into a network of participants make ongoing purchases of products and services, and recruit others to do the same, and they still others etc.—in endless chains of recruitment and personal consumption, in order to qualify for commissions and bonuses and to advance upward in the hierarchy of levels in a pyramid of participants."[4] Product purchases become the means of disguising or laundering investments in the scheme.

Taylor's definition of MLM brings out the following characteristics:

1. All the members who join the scheme by purchasing a product, becomes a distributor, authorized and motivated to recruit distributors, who are also motivated to do the same leading to an *endless chains of recruiters recruiting recruiters, without any concern for the market.*
2. Advancing in rank and position in the hierarchy of pyramid of "distributors" is based on timing of joining the scheme and recruitment, rather than on merit based appointment. A minimum purchase or recruitments is inevitable for such advancement. By creating an illusion of advancing in a hierarchy, members are lured into buying more products and recruiting more members. Most of the members do not understand that such committed purchases are the cost of running the business.
3. Sales are taking place only within the pyramid, and such sales are only for meeting the "Pay to Play" requirements. Few sales are made directly to consumers outside the pyramid at the actual market price. Overpriced products can be sold only to the incentivized members. The members frantically

attempt to build a downline and hence the working mechanism is that of an open pyramid scheme.

4. MLMs function on a "top weighted" pay plan. Here the upline participants get more benefit in the form of commissions and bonuses, than the person selling the product. Thus, as the incentive from retail sale is much less member will opt recruiting which offers more commissions. Bonus to senior leaders may take the form of group bonuses or larger discounts or higher commissions per sale.
5. Paying of commissions and bonuses to five or more levels of intermediaries is impossible. But, MLM companies make payments to an endless chain of intermediaries.

Tailor's definition is broad enough to cover the various aspects of MLM schemes such as chain enrollment, entry kit, maintenance of minimum self-consumption and illogical commission structure. Still from the enforcement angle further modification of the definition is imperative to develop some objective norms for detecting the presence of pyramid schemes in camouflaged version. He explained at length the excessive loss rate to majority of the members. But the overt reason behind this, i.e. compulsion to the lower level members to purchase unwanted products at the inflated price, need to be incorporated in the definition itself.

Need for a New Approach

Situation has become very complex with the emergence of more and more companies in the field which offer varieties of schemes that baffle both the investors and investigators. Absence of clear cut and objective norms make things easier for companies to claim legality for their schemes.

The first ever attempt to define Multi-Level Marketing in the Statute seems to be the one in the Kerala State Multi-Level Marketing (Control and Regulation) Bill. Here, the definition is, "multi-level marketing" or "direct selling" means marketing and sale of goods or providing services of a multi-level marketing entity through direct sellers or through direct sellers and distributors, otherwise than through shops, to the customers or consumers, generally in their houses or at their workplace or through explanation and demonstration of such goods and services at a particular place or by mail order sale."

The act of defining MLM and direct selling as synonymous is erroneous. The definition is insufficient from the enforcement angle as it does not incorporate any of the basic traits of the MLM such as, exorbitant price, unlimited recruitment of distributors, top weighted commission system, enrollment benefit, participation benefit etc. This definition would legalize the MLM, which has been held illegal by the courts, the worldover. However, this is an apt definition for direct selling.

Thus, it becomes imperative to develop a new definition of MLM that covers all the basic traits, which enables efficient enforcement to decimate the menace.

An examination of the various MLM schemes against which prosecution steps are initiated by the enforcement agencies, including those of the high profile conglomerates, shows that their basic content is over priced products and expansion of the network through recruitment.

The product selling MLMs claiming to be engaged in direct marketing are selling only eyewash items for hiding the deposits in money chains or are selling their products at a 10 fold of the actual market prices deceiving millions of consumers.

The new definition based on empirical analysis and facts established in the investigations should bring out the exploitative nature of MLM companies and their inherent working mechanism.

A New Definition of MLM

Multi-Level Marketing is a marketing scheme, for the sale of products or services, either fictitious one designed for token purpose or real ones bearing exorbitant price, by luring the purchasers to join the scheme after paying an entry fee in any form or even with no entry fee, with the offer of authority to enroll new members and easy money through a compensation plan, whereby a percentage of the sales proceeds are given to a chain of 4 or more layers of upline members, in the form of various incentives or commissions, contingent upon such enrollment, which can be in any pattern, or of any given width or depth.

This definition endeavours to bring out the following characteristics of the illegal scheme:

1. MLM is a scheme that lures the consumers of a product or service with the offer of fabulous gains of easy money, in the form of good compensation for the exorbitant price they pay, when they make further sales by enrolling new members. A large variety of incentives and commissions will be offered to the purchasers who become distributors.
2. The marketing scheme will be such that each member is authorized to enroll further distributors under him. The shape of the network need not necessarily be a pyramid and it can take any form depending on the permissible frontline direct recruitment under each member which is called width. The permissible downline expansion under each member is called the depth. Accordingly, there can be a variety of enrollment pattern such as binary plan, matrix plan, generation plan or a blend of different plans.
3. The marketing scheme need not necessarily include the sale of a product. The investment to money circulation scheme can be in the form of the premium for insurance, price for fictitious services.
4. MLM is a money circulation scheme like the pyramid scheme where the investment to the scheme is hidden in the price of the product or service. It can be done by designing totally worthless cheating products which are sold for record purpose only to hoodwink the investigators. Another way of doing this is selling a standard product at exorbitant price.
5. The price of product sold by the MLM companies will be very high as a percentage of this goes to a chain of upline members in the form of various commissions and incentives in a hierarchy of distributors. The products will be offered to the members at 7 to 15 fold of its actual market price as it should bring in sufficient income to make such payouts.
6. Only those schemes where commissions on sales are given to a chain of 5 or more layers of upline members need be considered as multi-level marketing.

7. Companies which sells the product at or near the market price cannot be considered to be illegitimate. For bringing down the price, the commissions to the endless chain of uplevel members are to be discarded. Also by reversing the commission rates, i.e. by paying more to the downline members who sells the products, with amount of commissions decreasing at each higher rank level, the scheme can be made fair to end consumers. Limiting the number of level to which commissions can be paid to a maximum of five is another way to bring down the price. The enrollment scheme will not work if these restrictions are enforced.
8. The schemes where the number of intermediaries between the manufacturers and the end consumers is less than five and where the sale is made at a rational price can be deemed to be a direct selling entity.

The above definition will help the investigators to easily identify an illegal Multi-Level Market scheme if it shows any of the following characteristics:

(a) Rampant sale of worthless products which do not have a real world market, through a chain referral system.
(b) Sale of products at incomparable prices of similar products available in the market supported by compensation plan.
(c) Any marketing plan which compels the members to make some Mandatory purchases of any product, or periodical subscription of accessory products or services during any specific period.
(d) Any incentive system which will prompt the members to purchase the products in a quantity which they can never sell i.e., the plans leading to inventory loading.
(e) Any plan which requires a new member to make initial cash payments for purchasing a starting kit including the sales literature like CDs or Pamphlets or any entry fee.
(f) Any plan where the company products are consumed only by the members of chain as no sales takes place outside the chain of distributors.

(g) Any scheme where the downline members are left with substantial unsold inventory upon cancellation of participation.

(h) Scheme where the purchase of products takes place even when the members do not have genuine demand for the products. Such purchase will be motivated by the desire to reach further stage in the marketing plan.

(i) Schemes which would fall down when participants do not make any purchase.

(j) Plans which does not require the members to make any real effort for sales after becoming a member to get rewards and commissions as they are entitled for the same out of the efforts of the downline members.

(k) Plans in which distributors are entitled to commission when new members are enrolled.

(l) The schemes in which more importance is given to recruitment of distributors rather than sale.

(m) A company which depicts an inflated picture of the earning of the members in their websites or in their business meets to lure new members.

Need for Continuous Watch

There has to be a system of continuous watch as Illegal pyramid schemes ripple across the world, attracting people by the irresistible psychological pull of quick and easy money offers. MLM Promoters often try to evade the consumer protection laws by claiming they are really selling a product.

Also it is not easy to identify the enrollment based MLM as the schemers have developed several occult models. The payment may be for a legitimate product. Instead of lump sum payment, extraction of money is made over a period of time. Thus, most of the members and even investigators fail to see it as an investment in a pyramid scheme.

Extravagant business meets, complicated pay plans, charismatic leaders, splendid offices, and donations to influential political parties and charitable causes are all the ways by which MLM promoters dupe regulators, legislators, and many in the media into believing they were legitimate.

Introduction of a more inclusive definition suggesting objective criterion for identifying MLM scheme is essential for bypassing the confusions created by the direct selling trade unions.

References

1. Richard Poe, 1995, *The New Era in Network Marketing,* Prima Publishing, New York, pp. 7-8.
2. Zig Ziglar with John P. Hayes, 2001, *Network Marketing for Dummies*, Hungry Minds, Inc.: New York, NY, p. 2.
3. Peter J. Vander Nat and William W. Keep, "Marketing Fraud: An Approach to Differentiating Multi-level Marketing from Pyramid Schemes."
4. *Taylor's e-book:* "The Case (for and) against Multi-level Marketing: The Complete Guide to Understanding and Countering the Effects of Endless Chain Selling and Product-based Pyramid Schemes." www.mlm-thetruth.com.

9
Categorisation of MLM Based on Enrollment Pattern

The fraudsters have designed several complicated versions of MLM by adopting different patterns of enrollment members into the scheme and different commission structure. This is done for confusing the enforcement agency and to claim legality for their designs. But none of this nefarious scheme discards the basic traits of pyramid model MLM, i.e., charging exorbitant price and chain recruitment of distributors.

The difference in the schemes are only in the nature of the tool of deception, devised for luring new members for ensuring sufficient new income to pay off the previous members.

MLM Concepts

The compensation plans of the companies are generally presented as an occult system in a complicated way with the help of several jargons like spill over, frontline width, depth, legs, point value, Business volume, commission etc. For deconstructing these intricate MLM plans, a clear understanding of these concepts is necessary.

Width and Depth

The number of persons placed by a subscriber directly under him is the "frontline" and it constitutes the width of the pyramid. The number of levels downwards under a subscriber up to which he is entitled for commission for the sale is the "downline" and it is also called the depth of the pyramid. Some compensation plans allows having infinite width such as the one in uni-level plan, generation plan, Stair Step

Breakaway plans etc. In some other plans depth will be unlimited, such as the one in binary plan.

Restricting the depth allowing unlimited width or restraining width allowing un-limited depth does not make justification for the scheme as both the ones leads to un-limited enrollment. However, the most dangerous scheme is the one which allows unlimited depth, meaning thereby unlimited layers of intermediary between the producer and the end consumer. Thus, arguing simply that the scheme is not a pyramid one does not give any legality to a scheme as the basic traits are the same.

Point Value

Instead of selling single money circulations scheme by hiding the deposit in the price of single product, companies devised new methodology for pyramid investment schemes simultaneously and to sell large number of products. This is accomplished by setting aside a specific percentage out of the price of a product for paying to the distributors at different levels. Each product carries a point value. In other words when a product is sold by a downline member in a network marketing scheme, large member of upline members are entitled to get different percentage from the price of the product. For example, in the Amway scheme, 49.5 per cent of the price of a product paid by the end consumers goes towards up level members in the form of various incentives and commission.

The commission of a member is determined by the volume of points accumulated by him through the sale of different products which carries different point value not only by him alone but by his entire downline. Therefore, each member will be tempted to build his own business team for earning higher commissions. Products with higher price normally carry higher point value. Normally, the companies allow higher point value to the worthless products designed solely for cheating purpose whereas quality products are allotted less point value.

Business Volume (BV): In some of the scheme point value is called Business Volume or Bonus Volume. The direct commission on sales going to the senior members of the scheme at different layers is specifically defined in the form of certain volume of points.

Different schemes use different types of point value for the calculation of total commission of members. This includes the following:

Self-Business Volume

Thus, every distributor is compelled to make some self-purchase every month to remain as "Active" in the system and in the absence of such self-purchase he will not be entitled to income. The total of the business volume of all the self-purchase and direct consumer sales made by a distributor together is called self BV. This compulsion to maintain minimum self-Business Volume, and sales on a subscription base leads the distributors to purchase unwanted products at over price. Amway compel for minimum 100 PV.

Team Business Volume (TBV)

The sum of point value of all the sales made by all the downline distributors under a leader is called his Team Business Volume. The total of Self BV + Team BV is called Group BV (GBV). This is the amount of points that is accumulated through the entire network of organization under a leader during a pay period. Group BV will be a parameter to assign ranks/designations/which decides percentage of income eligibility.

Carry Over Volume

This is also called the spillover volume. Some of the sales will not qualify the distributor for any commission during a particular pay period, if there is no corresponding pair matching or due to other conditions attached to the compensation plan. Such unmatched BV will be carried over to the next pay period. If the conditions are met during that period it will qualify the seller for commissions. The point value that is carried over from one billing cycle to another is called spill over volume.

Level Volume: The points accumulated by a member during a particular pay period is called the Level Volume.

Leg Volume: The points accumulated on one side of the genealogy is called the leg volume.

Variable Level Commission

The commission rate offered to the members at different levels in the hierarchy will be different in most of the plans. Whereas in the traditional marketing system the person responsible for sale is paid the highest point value in the MLM it is the other way round, i.e. the members at the higher level are entitled for a higher benefit than the lower level members. Variable Level Commission are particular to the plans named stair step Break Away, Uni Level and the Forced Matrix Plans.

Consistent Commission Rate: Some of the plans offer same rate of commission for each different level. Example is Binary Plan.[1]

Rank Advancement

A person who joins an MLM company as a distributor can gain new titles and earn recognition when the network under him expands beyond a certain level deep. As the organisation and the network grows, the individual member grows from simple distributor to a Diamond Director. For example in the Amway scheme there are 22 titles from the "silver producer" in the 1st level to "Founders Crown Ambassador in the 22nd level.

The above mentioned tools are used more or less in all the various marketing plan or else the difference between various MLM plan is only the difference in the application of these tools.

Major MLM Plans

A large variety of MLM plans are designed by the tricky gamers, using one or other of the above tools or a blunt of these. The important categories of MLM include: (1) Binary Plan, (2) Austratlian Binary, (3) Matrix Plan, (4) Revolving Matrix, (5) Generation Plan, (6) Break Away Plan, (7) Auto Filling Plan and (8) Growth Plan.

1. Binary Plan

The analysis of the pyramid scheme in the previous chapter is based on binary plan. Binary Plan can be applied both in Pyramid schemes and MLM. It *is the most familiar and widely accepted scheme all over the world.*

The buyer of a product is offered compensation by making him an agent of the company for selling the product, by enrolling him into a scheme. Every member has to sponsor minimum of 2 subscribers as their down layer, one in left and one in right on their own to make themselves eligible of binary pairing bonus. However, they can enroll more members in addition to the two in their left and right, but it will be placed to the extreme bottom vacancy on the chosen side.

The reward for a particular member in the scheme depends on the volume of sales made by the downline members and this depends on the spread of chain of sellers. Every sales carries a reward point named point value, business value etc. For ensuring expansion of the network in geometric progression, commissions are paid on business value matched on left and right of each person. This will give inducement to concentrate business on the weaker side.

Pair matching bonus is determined and calculated according to a formula. A given percentage of totals invested or business volume, matched left and right under each member will be given to him as binary matching commission and this is calculated at regular interval.

Binary matching commission is calculated in the following manner. Commission is calculated every month. Suppose Individual A is a top node and his total business value in one month is Rs. 130000 in the left side and Rs. 70000 on the right side. Now the binary matching is 70000. Only lower side is considered. Commission paid to Person A is 10 per cent of matching Point value i.e., 70000*10% = Rs. 7000, and the remaining unmatched business volume is fleshed out to the next month. Un-matched Point value is 130000 – 70000 = 60000. This un-matched PV will be carried forward to the next month. A ceiling will be set to the binary matching commission during a month. The weaker side is flushed out to next fortnight. When a new person is enrolled large number of persons in the upline is benefited as it leads to their binary matching of point value in some way or other.

Some constraints will be set on the binary matching commission during a particular billing period and this is called capping, trimming, flushouts etc.

The spread of network will be faster in a binary enrollment scheme than in any other model as only 2 people minimum is enough to succeed in the system. The scope of income to senior members is unlimited, if the duplication of team building progressed without interception, which is only an illusion. Thus, the number of person losing will be the highest in binary scheme making it the most exploitative, pervasive and dangerous of all investment schemes.

In a large team network, the people who stand on the top and build it, will have an opportunity of making huge money, fame and recognition, whereas the vast majority in the network loss their money. Proportion of members losing by making investment in a binary model pyramid scheme, regardless of the stage at which the scheme reached, will be around 87.5 per cent. Still requirement of recruitment of only 2 by each members, act as an invisible psychological pull luring the people into this fraud game.

Network building in a binary scheme which pre-supposes twice as many members in each new level compared to the immediate previous level, is in the following manner.

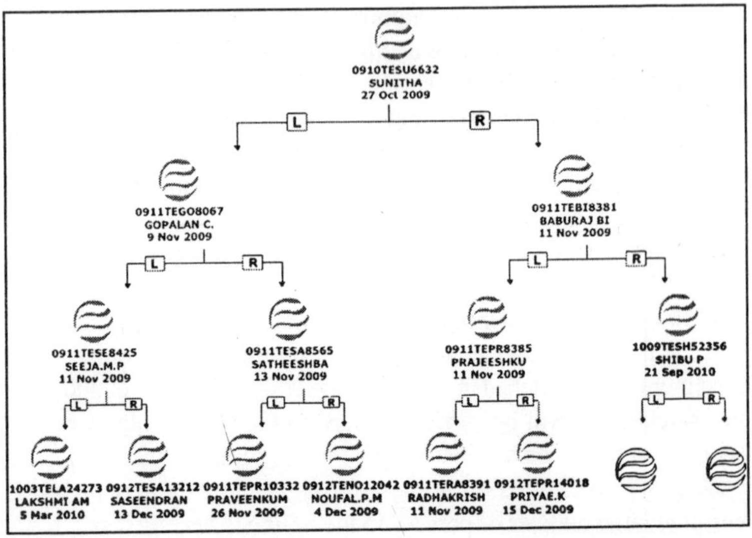

Fig. 9.1: Binary Tree View for User - 0910TESU6632 **Name Sunitha**

The price of the products sold by the MLM companies following binary enrollment pattern should be sufficient to make payouts to a large number of upline members as it allows unlimited downline. Thus, price would be 10 to 15 multiples of its actual market prices. It is an arithmetically infeasible and logically unviable scheme leading to fast market saturation.

Since, the beginning of binary plan business in India by Skybiz, the system of people recruitment in fraudulent schemes continued and millions of people who failed to recruit new members or could not succeed with proper duplication stood at lose. All the major scams in India were based on the business model of Binary plan. Speak Asia, ATCR, Stock Guru, Nano Excel, Tycoons Empire, Fine India, N mart etc... are all binary recruitment schemes.

2. Australian Two Up System

Two Up System is an Australian version of the fraudulent MLM plan. Here, the income from the first 2 recruits of every member will go to the immediate up-level member who recruited him. This refers to a marketing plan where the commission from the first two members recruited directly by a member are transferred to his sponsor. He is entitled to commission as his direct recruits goes further downline.

In *Australian Binary Plan* no pair matching is required. First two sales are qualifying sales and the third one is earning sales. Also, there is tremendous incentive for each of the recruits to pursue the 3rd enrollment or sale as this is the income coming to him.

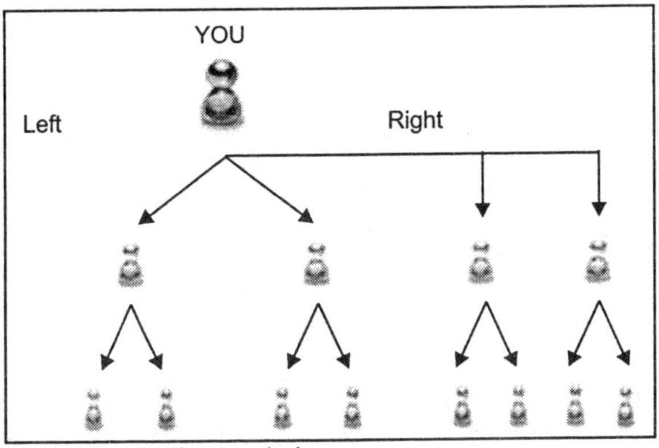

Source: www.dnbmlmsoftwaresolutions.com

Fig. 9.2

However, in this plan a member has option to refer more than 2 directs and can create additional parallel legs apart from left and right. The Australian binary plan allows unlimited front line though the downline is restrained to two layers.

Though the downline keeps growing, a particular member is entitled to commission only from the sale of second layer downline.

The system does not discard the unlimited enrollment feature of MLM as member can go for building unlimited front line directly under him. It maintains the "endless chain" feature of the pyramid scheme. New recruits should make the first two qualifying sales forfeiting commissions to an upline sponsor. Later recruits find it impossible to make benefit and goes victim to the purchase of product at inflated price. 2-up recruits who fail to recruit two others become in effect the downline of someone above them.

The prospects of continued sale and expansion of network of members will soon meet with a halt as market saturation will be fast in this scheme. So, the recruits at the bottom level lose *all* their money.

This also is a pyramid where Investments in the scheme are typically covered behind the price of the overpriced products. The price of the products sold by the companies following the Australian binary plan will be too much high as the scheme is designed in such a manner that the commission from just 4 members recruited by the immediate downline is supposed to fetch an income which will more than compensate each member.

This plan is very pervasive as it offers exponential growth in the income levels for the person at the top at the cost of the hapless victims at the bottom level.

3. The Matrix Plan

MLM Companies run a numerous variety of matrix plan where the difference is only on the extent to which enrollment of new members under an existing member is allowed. Accordingly, different matrix plans allow the members a set width and depth under him where, width stands for the frontline or number of members who can be directly recruited under a member and depth stands for the downward layers upto which a member is given commission when fresh enrollment is made. The width and depth of the plan distinguishes one from another. For example a 3×5 plan suggests that only a maximum of 3 frontline distributors can be sponsored by a member and potential to earn commissions up to 5 levels deep.

After filling the limited width, distributors are encouraged to assist their downline members and this helps pervasive proliferation of the fraudulent scheme. After crossing limitation new recruits will be positioned under any of the existing downline distributors. This "spill over" process is common to other plans like Binary Plan. New distributors were automatically placed into the next available position in some plans whereas in some others distributors are given option to decide where they want to position the new entrants.

The genealogy of a 3×3 matrix is shown below:

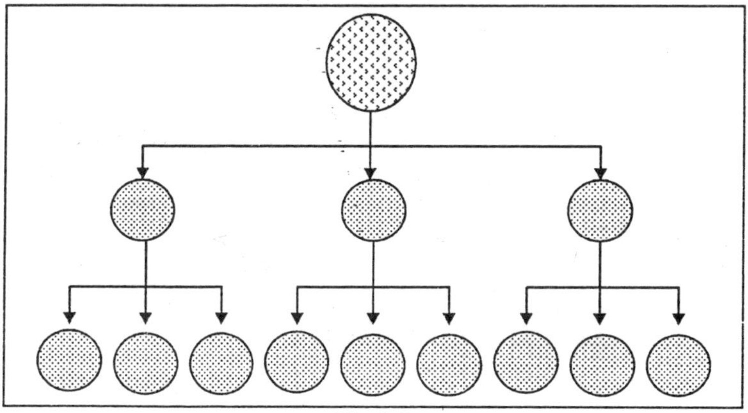

Fig. 9.3

The proportion of members losing in the matrix plan also will be very high. The general equation for finding out the proportion of members losing in the scheme to the total members of the scheme can be modified as follows:

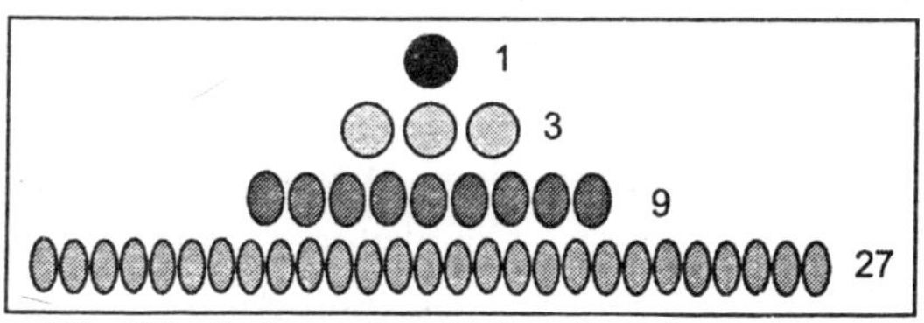

Fig. 9.4: Each new level brings in 3 times as many

At the Nth level down from the top, there are 3^N members

The total Number of members or the Nth level plus all levels above $= 3^N + \frac{3^N - 1}{2}$

$$\frac{\text{Members Losing Money}}{\text{Total Members}} = \frac{3^N}{3^N + \frac{3^N - 1}{2}}$$

Note: We assume that each new member brings in 3 more. Also, at the very bottom level, members lose their money

We simplify this fraction to get

$$\frac{3^N}{3^N + \frac{3^N - 1}{2}} = \frac{3^N}{\frac{2 \times 3^N}{2} + \frac{3^N - 1}{2}} = \frac{3^N}{\left(\frac{2 \times 3^N + 3^N - 1}{2}\right)}$$

$$= \frac{2 \times 3^N}{2 \times 3^N + 3^N - 1} = \frac{2 \times 3^N}{3 \times 3^N - 1}$$

$$\frac{\text{Members Losing Money}}{\text{Total Members}} = \frac{2 \times 3^N}{3 \times 3^N - 1}$$

If we neglect the -1 in the denominator, we get $\frac{2 \times 3^N}{3 \times 3^N} = \frac{2}{3}$ which is less than $\frac{2 \times 3^N}{3 \times 3^N - 1}$

This means $\frac{\text{Members Losing Money}}{\text{Total Members}} > \frac{2}{3} = 66.6\bar{6}\%$

The companies following matrix plan generally restrains only frontline and allows unlimited downline. Though there were a few companies which followed this plan, it is not so rampant now-a-days. The following companies have followed this plan.

1. Tolido Marketing Pvt. Ltd.—Hyderabad (2000)
2. Target Networks—Hyderabad (2000)
3. Suguna Consumer Services—Warangal (2001)
4. One Way Marketing—Coimbatore (2001)
5. Faith Line Marketing—Belguam (2001)

4. The Generation Plan

The Multi-Level Marketing plan which allows maximum number of frontline members is named Generation Plan. A very fast expansion of the network of sellers is possible as an existing member can recruit any number of new distributors under him. The Generation plan is also termed as Uni-level Plan, Sunflower Plan, Staircase Plan, Gap Commission Plan etc. but the genealogy structure and enrollment pattern are the same.

Though, only two members can be enrolled under each member in a traditional pyramid scheme, Generation Plan is more dangerous and viral as an existing member can enroll any number of members under him as his frontline.

The network of the companies which adopted this plan has spread the worldover. This plan with little variation is adopted by the companies like Amway, Tiens, Oriflame, Tupperware, Herbalife etc.... Basing on a stipulated per cent of Margins available from each product/service rendered, the incomes are offered to a chain of up-line members.

Anyone may sponsor as many as possible on their own. This plan envisages a minimum level of self-purchase by each member, to make himself eligible for bonuses. The genealogy structure of generation plan is as follows:

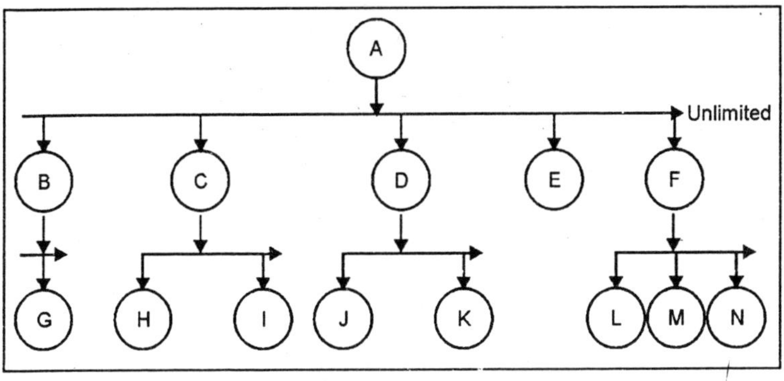

Fig. 9.5: Team Building Structure Illustration

The commission offered to the members in different layers will be different and it progresses cumulatively, according to the total value of group business. The percentage of commissions offered to the leaders at the top of the network will be high whereas in the traditional business the retailer gets the highest percentage of commission.

Distributor 10%	Team Leader 15%	Manager 18%	Senior Manager 21%	General Manager 24%	Vice President 27%	President 30%
10000 GBV	25000 GBV	50000 GBV	1 lakh GBV	3 lakhs GBV	10 Lakhs GBV	20

Fig. 9.6: Staircase Commissions Structure

Companies following this pattern is found selling products at 10 fold of the actual market price as huge amount is required to make payout to differentup stair members. Some sales are made to the consumers outside the pyramid at the rate shown as MRP. But this will be an insignificant proportion of the total sale.

But sales to the new recruits, who form the outer layer from the epicenter or lower strata, will be at 7 to 15 fold of the MRP. A special price called 'distributor price' is offered to the registered distributors of the company after discount which enable senior leaders to gain margin.

Calculation Method

The commissions are disbursed generally once in a month. The following steps are followed to determine each distributor's eligible ranks and percentage of commission.

Every distributor is supposed to maintain their self BV to remain active in the business and for becoming eligible for commissions. When the rank grows, the self BV required may be more in some companies.

A distributor's rank is determined on the basis of his TBV, and higher commission percentages are given to those with higher TBV. Direct commissions are given on the basis of Self BV.

In addition, there may be many promotional programmes time to time to promote sales. Posh business meets will be held for launching of new products.

The gain of commissions for the distributors depends on the difference in ranks with their direct downline. This kind of plan prompts every distributor to make maximum direct recruitment of distributors and to pursue a career of continued salesmen-ship.

Extremely inflated price of the product, inventory loading, i.e., purchase of unwanted products to make oneself eligible for a particular commission rate, market saturation are all the unfair attributes of this scheme.

5. The Breakaway Plan

The Stair Step Breakaway Plan is another variety of Generation Plan. Each distributor is only allowed to sponsor one level of distributors, whereas there is no limit to the width of frontline members. After reaching a qualifying stage members are allowed to breakaway from the upline and can act as an independent business owner with downline only. Stair step breakaway plan aims at recruiting large number of frontline distributors, who personally consume or sell product and then encourage others to do the same.

Breaking away from upline gives a higher commission rate to the individuals. By breaking away, the volume of commission of upline members no longer flows. When best customers are lost they will concentrate on new team building.

As distributors breakaway, the original sponsor is still entitled to earn a small percentage from each breakaway distributor's efforts. This is referred to as an *override commission.* Each breakaway organisation is referred to as a *generation* and leaders are entitled to earn an override commission on all of their breakaway generations. This override commission would be a small fraction of the commissions they were earning previously.

The distributors in the downline also will qualify for breakaway in the Stair Step Breakaway Plan. Breakaway causes a dent in the short-term income, of senior leaders but creating a number of breakaway groups will help earn a long-term residual income.

The staggering loss rate and viral nature of the breakaway plan is explained by Tailor as "In a breakaway system, the levels in the hierarchy are made up, not of individual participants, but of breakaway organizations (or pyramids)—groups of participants who have met requirements to breakaway, allowing a small commission override from all participants in the breakaway unit. So, in a breakaway system, a hierarchy of six levels is actually six levels of *groups* of participants, which makes it a constellation of pyramids within a giant mega-pyramid—with most of the payout going to TOPPs."

It causes extreme loss rate as the top-level distributors are supported by a downline of several groups who actually loses money, after subtracting purchases and other expenses. All the groups together constitute a pyramid. The following domains are doing business using this extreme exploitative plan:

www.AMWAY.com—USA
www.Herbalife.com—USA
www.Tianshiindia.co.in—China/India

6. Revolving Matrix Plan

Revolving Matrix Plan is quite distinct from the remaining plan. Generally, in all the referral marketing plan, the new members are following the upline member, but in revolving matrix system, a down-line member can supersede the sponsor on the basis of more and early sales than the sponsor. Anyone may sponsor as many new recruits as possible to make himself eligible for bonuses.

Revolving Matrix Structure Illustration

There will be 2 boards of 4 levels depth. First Board is called Qualifying Board and second one is Executive Board. The first 3 levels are prefilled in each board and the bottom line of fourth level, with vacant 8 boxes, will be open for the entry of new members. Every new member in the company will be entered in the first vacancy of fourth level left to right.

When all the 8 vacancies are filled, the member on the Top at first level will get Income from Qualifying Board and also moves to Executive Board. Further, the remaining 14 members in the qualifying board will now form into 2 new qualifying boards with 7 IDs in each.

While shuffling and forming the new Qualifying Boards, there is a system to rearrange the users in the format of 2-1-0. Out of 14 balance users in the system those who made 2 sponsoring first will be taken into consideration and will be placed at the top.

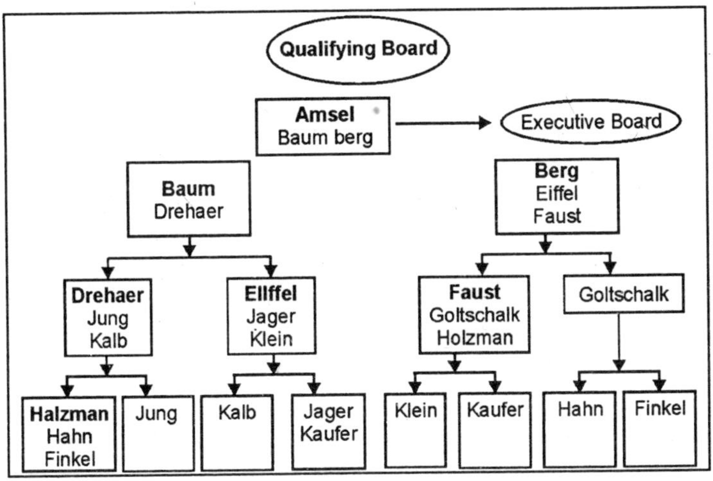

Fig. 9.7

When all the 8 vacancies on the bottom line got filled up, the first member Amsel on the top will get a commission and also moves to Executive Board. Further 2 new Qualifying boards will be formed as below as per the above explained formula.

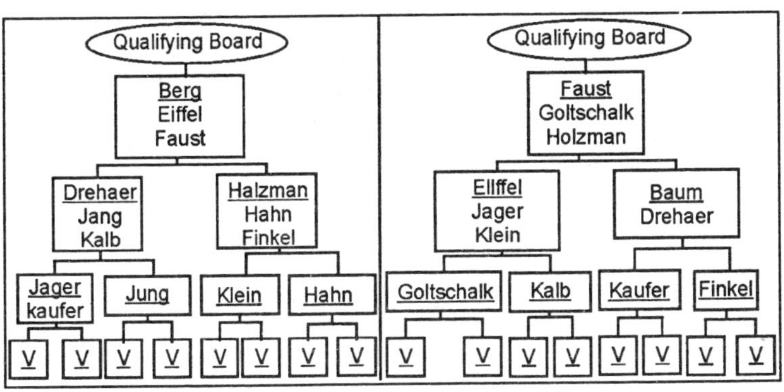

Fig. 9.8

The members who move to Executive Board crossing the qualifying board also follow the same methodology in a new board. They will get a Bonus along with a re-birth in the Executive Board placement followed by his sponsor or senior at the latest vacancy. This keeps rotating for ever again and again. A person who makes more and early sales will lead fast in the system and get commissions sufficiently.

Case Studies

This kind of plan was first brought by a company named Club Freedom, Australia then adopted by many other companies across the world like TVI Express etc. TVI Express, launched by Mr. Tarun Trikka, had done business across the world and there were nearly two lakh members from India.

7. The Auto Filling Matrix Plan

The Auto filling Matrix Plans are basically computer system filled top to bottom, left to right in a predefined 2X or 3X formula. Here irrespective of the person who sponsors a member his position in the pyramid will automatically come in the first blank node, i.e. the system will automatically fill the pyramid. Here the sales will be placed in a format of sequential, irrespective of the position of sponsor in the chain. Generally, in any other kind of plan, the enrollment will be below the sponsor, but here the sales will automatically fill up pyramid format. A member will get commission, when the nodes under him are filled by virtue of anybody enrolling new members.

The companies following this plan create a boom within a short period and will be winding up the operation after siphoning off the accumulated funds.

Anyone may sponsor as many members for becoming eligible for bonuses. The genealcgy structure will be a typical pyramid as there is no blank node in this plan. This is nothing but a binary plan. Early to join, higher will be the income. There is no room for selling skills and hard work in this plan. People who joined at the top will make big money, and vast majority will lose in this system also. Fast market saturation and failure to expand the scheme beyond a level will cause losses to the downline members.

M/s. Remo Marketing Pvt. Ltd., Ahmedabad (2004), had done 40 lakh sales in 5 months and created all time record in India and finally, landed up as big scam. Mr. Zarin Rana, owner of the company, was grilled by the Gujarat Police and is facing prosecution. The company presented 2 Benz cars to celebrities Mr. Amitabh Bachchan and Mr. Kapil Dev during an event, which was seized by Police which drew National Media hype on this subject.

8. Growth Plan

Growth plans are a new breed of plans that are invoked in Indian MLM Industry. Member will get percentage share of the growth in the company. *Growth plan* claims that members are getting benefit of the company's growth. Monthly income is based on company's growth. The growth rate will be different in different months and there are options to see company's growth from month to month. The so called growth is expected to come from the enrollment of members and sale at exorbitant price.

It is a variant of the 'Auto Filling' systems. Usually any Auto Filling system, begins from the first ID and develops the downline either on his own or by the company through 'Auto Filling'. But the Growth plans starts with more than one ID.

The scheme can be started with 50 or 100 IDS as frontline. Here the customer does not have an option to see the level at which he is getting enrolled. Payouts are offered to a member only when the depth of network goes beyond a specific level like 10 or 12. Till then only nominal percentage commission will be offered. It requires huge number of members and normally the sales will not be sufficient to support the payout.

Those joining the scheme at the initial stage will be benefited fast but the later entrants will have to go without any payout.

The companies need to make payouts only once the downline reaches 12th level which is rather impossible. There will be a huge margin for the company and the fund flow would also be huge. By the time the promoters realise what's happening, it would be too late and they would have burnt their fingers by then.

It is also known as doubling scheme and has flourished in South India. Schemes like 'Swiss Cash' followed this plan. Several companies mushroomed in Andhra Pradesh like 'Maha Life', Happy Life, Diamond Life, Genius, Vennela, and so on following this plan.

9. Para Banking Schemes

Para Banking is a business whereby private or public limited registered companies recruit agents and develop a network, and accept investments from the customers against the security of land possessed by the company. It operates like a banking company and offers to double the investment in 2 or 3 years. Fixed deposits, and recurring deposits are also accepted with a handsome offer of returns in short span comparatively earlier than any other scheduled bank in India.

Funds are collected by selling units of land at a given price. There will be an offer of buy-back by the companies after two or three years at double the price. The companies purchase some barren, or marshy or un-demarcated low quality land. Money is collected mainly on installment basis and registration certificate of land will be issued after completing a given premiums of installment payments. Customers never get a chance for verifying the quality of land situated in the far off state in their name.

The following factors help the companies to survive and prolong in the field doing the cheating operations.

A member will be qualifying to earn the offered rate of return only if he makes payment of installment for continuous period of 5 or 10 years. Nearly 40 per cent of the members dropouts from the plan, as they default on the premium payment for the given period. They normally forget about the one or two installments of payment when it matures. Thus, the companies need not have to pay them.

Almost 30 per cent of the greedy investors go for reinvestment when companies offer new schemes and thus, actual payment is not required.

Only around 30 per cent people claim their money on maturity and hence, the companies never feel the burden of meeting the offered returns.

Land units are sold against undivided property. Sales will be several multiples of the actual extent of land possessed by the companies. For example, Company having a land bank of 100000 square yards sell plots in multiples of 100 square yards and total sale will be to the tune of 4 to 5 lakhs square yards. In one case, the total land allotted by the so-called real estate company was 67 times more than the land owned by the company.

The companies doing this illegitimate business have developed special *modus operandi* to hoodwink the enforcement agencies.

Companies are getting registered with Registrar of Companies as a public limited company and further approach RBI with an application for NBFC licence.

Due to inadequate eligibility like statutory requirement and collateral security, the RBI rejects the application and denies to give NBFC licences.

The companies will approach High Court of the respective state seeking stay order on the rejection and review again by showing some more credentials of the company.

The High Court allows interim stay order and subsequent proceedings are dragged for years. But the companies will start the business and accumulate funds from the public through multi-levels of commission agents.

RBI's job is over once they reject the application and they will not keep in any surveillance these kind of companies unless otherwise a written compliant received by them. This gap is being used by many companies and managed to collect hundreds of crore of public money unauthorized.

These companies claim doing the business of real estate, or developing of agricultural land or scientific rearing of livestock etc. Three of such companies had 21 lakh members, each of whom gave substantial deposits to these companies. On paper, the so-called Real Estate companies were allotting land to these individuals but in reality they were only accepting deposits on the assurance of high rate of interest.

Funds are floated by issuing Preference Shares without obtaining sanction from SEBI and agents are appointed offering stake in the real estate investment fund. They will get commission when new people are signed up. Suppose an agent signs on 4 people, when each of them signs on another 4, the original agent receives commission for 16 people. Money is initially raised at hefty interest rates, and with attractive periodic prizes and gifts. There is a highly incentivized structure of brokers or agents.

High interest, agents commissions, the luxurious business meetings and pompous parties makes the working cost very high. No business can sustain such staggering commitment and the schemes are destined to doom in the absence of application of some tools for out right cheating or theft.

The companies posed as engaged in real estate or infrastructure development business uses a series of deceptive tools. Only minimum of real estate business is done. They devise some projects and blow it out of proportion through the media. After reserving a 10 per cent of the plot in their possession in the middle for the project the remaining part will be sold at several fold in the wake of the hype created by the project. Once the sale is over they vanish abandoning the so-called projects. Even by these cheating, they cannot generate revenue from these projects for making returns to the investors. Most of the companies survive the business only depending upon the fresh investments received every month.

The companies doing Para Banking business also go for enrollment of agents for the purpose of making collections. There is large number of agents like the one in pyramid scheme or MLM. The team of agents will be recruited and are promoted as the agents under them expand. Remunerations, incentives and bonuses, increase with every stage promotion. A minimum of 40—50 per cent of the total collection is required for meeting commission of agents at multi-levels. Then expected returns generation is impossible with remaining 50 per cent collection. Thus, though involvement of money circulation scheme is overt in these type of plans also, precautions are made by these companies to hide the enrollment aspect of the business.

This kind of para banking business is very familiar in India since last 2 decades by various notorious companies like Peerless, SAHARA, PACL etc.... Gradually hundreds of companies doing business in this format has mushroomed and many of them collapsed without making much advancements due to reckless money management.

Companies doing this *modus* of collection have stormed the Indian capital market by collecting funds beyond imaginations. PACL, SAHARA, Smriddi Jeevan, Agri Gold etc. are a few of the companies which collected more than 1000 crore.

Case Study

1. *PACL*—It is an Indore based, Delhi operated company doing business since last 15 years, having asset worth of Rs. 75,000 crore.

Their recent balance sheet exposed that a deposit amount of nearly Rs. 5000 crore are lying unclaimed in the company account.

The company later changed its name to Witel See Marketing Ltd.[2]

Samruddi Jeevan—It is a Pune based 10 years old company and it collected nearly Rs. 10,000 crore. They established various projects and business with public money.

Agrigold—The collection of this Vijayawada (AP) based 8 years old company went beyond Rs. 3,000 crore.

These companies do not have proper statutory eligibility to the business to make public collection. But corporate lobbying is being practiced for managing the situation

10. Other HYIP

Besides the business plans in the above described formats, the con men have developed several High Yielding Investment Plans, other than enrollment based schemes or MLM. Cheating are rampant in the name of Forex Trading, market manipulations etc. Any investment business like share trading, commodity trading, real estate, sale of insurance or banking products which offers 12 per cent to 20 per cent per annum is regular and reasonable. But the offers are sky level and greedy and gullible flock there and perish like swarm of flies to the candle. All the high yielding programmes make payments of offered returns in the initial times to create credibility and to show off the glossy success stories of the early members.

Problem will arise for paying returns to the investors when the collection goes equal or less than the previous month, and outflow crosses the inflow. Liquidity crisis leads to close down and run away by cheating the people.

Several of the companies operate solely through virtual web based software, private bank accounts, and cash payments through third party agencies without any registration or legitimacy.

References

1. *http://www.network-marketing-business-school.com/compensation-plan.*
2. http://www.witalsee.com

10
MLM—Chasing a Mirage

The easy money offer made by the Multi-Level Marketers will soon prove to the members to be a mirage which can never be attained. Those who fail in the chase are tuned to accept their failure. The companies adopt large variety of tools for creating an unending passion in the citizens to join this mad race. In every MLM scheme, after the initial pandemonium and brouhaha the popular delusion subsidies, throwing away the millions in the downline to abject pauperism.

Still the instances of successfully conducting prosecution steps against the promoters of such schemes are very rare as they have some innate mechanism for surviving the clutches of enforcement.

The enforcement agencies tend to exempt the product based Multi-Level marketing from prosecution in the wake of the pressure tactics played by the direct selling associations. It is a direct onslaught on the democratic rights of the consumers.

The very mechanism of multi-level marketing with close relatives or friends at the immediate up-level, with whom only a member will have business deal is a well crafted protection against launching of criminal complaint against the leaders in the scheme. Thus, the end consumers never tend to raise complaint against the persons who enrolled them. The risk of being prosecuted by police is less, as the members in any scheme generally enrolls their relatives and friend for initial period. Thus majority of the members will be reluctant to file petition against their immediate upline.

The only solution for overcoming this is a compulsion in the law making it mandatory for the police officers to initiate *suo motu* legal action against such schemes.

Judging in terms of the number of victims, loss rate and other social and economic damages, MLM is the most exploitative and deceptive of all the con schemes. But the enforcement is found fumbling for want of a clear understanding of the various categories of MLM. The cooperate deception goes to the extent of presenting their own scheme as "Genuine MLM" depicting all the others as illegitimate. Corporate lobbying in some jurisdiction went to the extent of exempting MLM from prosecution.

The con artistes have devised a variety of deceptive tools for prolonging market saturation. These let the Multi National Corporations to argue that MLM is not a pyramid scheme. Ultimate collapse like the one in a pure Pyramid scheme can be avoided in an MLM as there is no offer of repayment in the absence of downline enrollment.

The net effect is that millions of end users of the product are lured to purchase the products at several folds of their actual market price and does not get any compensation for this. An array of tools are devised to ensure continued sale of goods or services to consumers.

Direct Selling associations are pushed to defend the cause of MLM. The exploitation of consumers and mass recruitment towards this out right gambling are argued to be legitimate income opportunities and public opinion is distorted in that way.

Those who quit the scheme again re-enter the scheme or else will be replaced by new recruits MLM members at the top can maintain their positions and high income levels by aggressively following the cheating methodology.

Despite numerous instances, people still fall for 'Double the Money' schemes offered by Fly-by-night operators. The senior leaders of the schemes misguide people to join such companies. They join atop the pyramid so that they can take the biggest share of the loot, but play victim when the company closes down. Later they repeat this with some other companies or start with a new one on their own.

John M. Taylor terms the deceptive survival strategy adopted by the product selling MLM for avoiding market collapse as '8 R's of MLM durability'.[1]

Re-pyramiding

To counter the saturation in sales, the companies keep changing the products or introducing new edition of the old products and keep building new pyramids. *Re-pyramiding is initiating a new pyramid in respect of an altogether new product or in a new geographical area, especially by accessing a foreign economy while the existing pyramid is about to collapse.*

Even the scheme will be presented in the name of a new company, i.e., putting the old wine in new bottle is part of total deception. Quixtar is the new name assumed by Amway in the United States. At the same time they kept the brand name in overseas market. The scheme is adapted to access different countries for taking advantage of the loopholes in their law. *Diversification of product line is resorted to by the MLM Companies*. Global Market saturation also will happen when it is difficult to find virgin market.

Appearing in the Garb of Direct Selling

MLM everywhere is appearing in the garb of direct sales when an imminent collapse is anticipated. They tend to misguide the media and legislators that they are engaged in direct sales and that the anti- Pyramid laws are not applicable to them. A fraction percentage of the wrongful gain made over decades is sufficient to blow through media advertisements. Trade Unions form direct selling associations and resort to various pressure tactics and succeed in exonerating exploitative scheme from prosecution. This is a globally accepted MLM manipulation. Even when endless chain of middlemen takes away more than 70 per cent of the price of products, they will shamelessly claim that they eliminate middle men.

MLM can never claim to be direct selling. *Direct Marketing is sale of products by the manufacturers direct to the end consumers. In direct marketing company bears the cost of stocking inventory and no purchase is required but in MLM initial and ongoing purchases are essential to qualify for commissions and inventory cost are borne by the distributors. Commissions will be high in direct marketing to the limited number of persons who actually makes the sales but it is the other way round in MLM. The override commissions to the higher-ups take away a major part of the price of a product in MLM. The thrust in direct marketing is door to door sales to end consumers and in MLM it is for recruiting the new distributors.*

MLM promoters go to great lengths to make it appear that their revenues come from direct selling of products, which is simply not the case.

1. The term Direct Selling presupposes that there is no intermediary between the Manufacturer and End Consumer. As the Manufacturer sells goods/articles without any intermediary avoiding the costs involved in such distribution, the consumer is expected to get such goods at a minimum price. Thus in direct selling both the consumer and manufacturer will be the beneficiaries.
2. MLM it is claimed is a form of direct selling, which has a long history of independent selling by "door-to-door salesmen" and of selling to friends, neighbours, and family members. It is this person-to-person relationship selling that is one of its great strengths.
3. But the truth is that MLM should more properly be considered chain or pyramid selling, as few sales are made to customers outside its network of distributors.
4. Also, we see the fallacy of the claim of MLM promoters that they are removing the "middle man" in their marketing system. Actually, in an MLM, middlemen may number in the thousands in multiplying downlines.
5. Without even a genuine need for a product, the MLM members will buy products to qualify for profits from recruiting others. Retailing to close circle involve restriction of choice, and consumers face the inconvenience of pressure from friends and relatives.

Starting Kit and Repeated Purchase

It is customary in all the MLM schemes to make collection from the new entrant a specific fee by giving a starting kit which contains the pamphlets of the cheating scheme. These are the "Tools for success", contained in books, audio programmes etc. to aid new recruits in "building their business."

Tapes and follow-up pack will be left to the members to duplicate, and teach. They will cheerfully congratulate you for becoming new business owners. They will promise to help you succeed. The tapes and literature will be full of motivation and inspiration. You may not understand the mechanics of how the business will work. Your upliners are there to reassure you until you are more conversant with the scheme. For this business consultancy you need not have to pay. This mentorship programme will be appeals as successful people leading the way. The literature will advise to invite double the number of people you actually expect to come to have a successful meeting. The "inviting" techniques involve avoiding words like the name of company, "products" or "selling" in the phone at the time of inviting.

Besides this compulsion to maintain a minimum self-business value to remain active in the scheme will create some market. Even selling the products on a subscription basis also leads to unwanted purchase. A downline member will be relieved from the cob-web only when he decides to withdraw from the scheme. Taylor points out "The minimum 100 PV (personal volume) for Quixtar (Amway) participants was "roughly equal to $260/month ($3,120 per year)." And "because Quixtar's overpriced products are not saleable to anyone except distributors who are buying to qualify for bonuses. Quixtar distributors' earnings are a direct function of how much product they and their downline consume. The more internal consumption and the larger the downline, the higher will be the bonus."

Escalating incentives to continue purchasing products to qualify for higher commissions rates and/or ever-higher levels in the hierarchy of participants often lead "distributors" to hyper-consume products or to give away.

Euphoria of Success Stories

They will project the incredible wealth they earned and will show off the enviable lifestyle *via* the Business. The dropouts from the scheme are expected to be substituted by constant recruitment of new member and this will be fuelled by the euphoria created by the success stories of top members who harvested from the scheme. The losses following the collapse of MLM companies are shifted to such dropouts. A revolving door of recruits can replace dropouts to some extent through aggressive enrollment by making fabulous income opportunity.

Indoctrination into MLM

In the very beginning, the members will be invited to the flamboyant business meets required to inculcate ideas, attitudes and strategies for conditioning him to accept MLM as the be all and end all and ultimate business truth. Every MLM business meets are so tuned to mould such a mind set of implicit obedience so that no body go for critically examining the viability of the schemes. He will be assigned a starting kit consisting of some booklets, cassettes and CDs all aimed at brain-washing the gullible into MLM business.

The author of merchants of deception rightly puts it: *" My sponsor and the rest of my upline referred to this system for success continually. It involved the ongoing weekly purchase of cassette tapes, books for daily reading, videos, CD-ROMs, and tickets for the monthly seminars and frequent training sessions. What we didn't realize until much later is that, in essence, this system of success was little more than a gradual and unrelenting indoctrination. We heard a college professor, who also happened to be a Direct Distributor, declare that this was the greatest educational system he had ever found. "*

The top achievers praise the system as the magical way of becoming wealthy. When all those speak of the same system everybody will get tempted. Skilled MLM orators speak to thousands of distributors praising the virtue of top upline leaders. They are depicted to be men of charity, principle, character, courage, and integrity. Enrolling into the fraudulent scheme is presented as a charity work of helping the poor to grow financially. The scheme is presented as a system to second to none and will persuade the members to stay with it and believe in it.

A new mind set is created to accept MLM ideology and to accept their failure. "Most of the victims in the con game rationalize their failure as incapability on their side and such self-deception continues until they run out of resources and quit. They rationalize their failure in saying that they did not strive much."[2] The friends and relatives will be direct recruiters of each member and this always prompts for self-incrimination when they land up in trouble and failure.

Sale Outside Pyramid

Retailing of products outside the pyramid claimed by the MLM as a ground for evading prosecution is only an illusion as there is no mechanism to review this rule. It is only an eyewash to misguide the enforcement agency. In some of the ruling stipulations are made to legalize the scheme and this include:

> (1) 70 per cent of the product sales are to be made to non-participants; (2) Distributors must prove a sale to a minimum of ten customers each month, and; (3) There has to be buy back provisions.

These provisions laid down by Federal Trade Commission in America is only an abortive attempt to set right the industry which is built on the fluid foundation. These provisions cannot be enforced and are paid only lip service by the MLM companies. Quixtar has revealed recently in a court proceeding that only *3.4 per cent of sales were made outside pyramid. MLM system does not promote direct sales* at *retail prices*.

Extensive Public Relation Works

There will be a public relation department for all the MLM companies and wherever adverse news or prosecution is initiated, the team will immediately rush there and will brief the merits of their scheme to the correspondents of media and bureaucrats. The innate quality of the scheme is such that it can easily create confusion and are designed to falsely overcome the legal provisions. For ensuring social acceptance and legitimacy for the fraudulent schemes, MLMs resort to sponsoring of several highly visible programmes. Inviting top political leaders for their business meeting and family get together and marketing of celebrities speeches at MLM conventions are all deceptive tools of the game.

They go on propagating that the methods of referral marketing are in the curriculum of several universities and even MLM leaders are honoured by Universities and civic groups. No standard management experts mentioned MLM or multi-level or network marketing as an arena for professional sales-persons. No writing on salesmanship have included MLM as a form of selling. Apparently, MLM is respectable only to those doing it.

Senior Leaders Playing Victim

The perpetrators in these schemes pretend to be victims when the scheme collapses. But they will create frenzy for joining first whenever new scheme is launched. These senior leaders provide all the logistic support for newer and newer cheating designs when one collapses. There are several instances of top leaders themselves lodging complaint for avoiding large number of complaints against them by members in the lower strata.

The top leader in the pyramid who enjoyed the benefit of great reward will misrepresent the quality of products and will present the scheme as a business opportunity.

Refund Policy

Wherever MLM or Pyramid scheme becomes scandal, con men come forward to dodge the consumers with the offer of repurchase or refund of the sales proceeds. It will not have any practical manifestation as MLM subscribers are conditioned to accept their "failure" and never admit the fraud nature of the merchandise scheme. Thus, offer of refund for unused purchase within one month does not actually give any protection to the consumers.

Unique Products

The products offered by the MLM companies are of a particular sort which never allows the consumers for a comparative quality analysis or price worthiness and these fall in the category "pills, potions and lotions". MLM products include 'For ever Living Products', skincare and health supplements, jewels, bags, watches and wallets. A large client base is created for these products propagating the esoteric qualities.

The companies through their promotional literature, audio and video material and meetings, motivate people to get enrolled as members by buying a product and as is inevitable, majority of the members would not be able to benefit. An analysis of the price list of various MLM companies show that the sale of product as part of enrollment is at or nearly 10 fold of the actual retail price of the product.

References

1. John M. Taylor—*The Case against Multi-level Marketing as an Unfair and Deceptive Practice.*
2. Robert L. Fits Patrick.

11
Scam Ways of Amway

With thousands of criminal charges faced by it, spread across several nations, the name of Amway has become synonymous with scam, deception and fraud over the several decades since its inception. It is the oldest and largest of all the MLM companies and became notorious for corporate lobbying and manipulative tactics using political influence.

When a Canadian court called for the production of copies of all law suits filed against Amway Corporation and its directors three decades back, the Amway's attorney responded saying that: "The request imposes an undue burden is that the number of lawsuits filed against Amway Corporation and/or Richard DeVos and/or Jay Van Andel for the past ten years represents literally thousands of lawsuits, with the file on each lawsuit varying from several pages to entire rooms filled with documentation."[1]

This brings out the number criminal charges faced by Amway company in various countries in 1985. With the elapse of three more decades' of thefts by deception and consequent scandal worldwide, Amway is the world's number one mugger in terms of the number of cases faced by it.

USA

In its own home land Amway had to fight a series of lawsuits. One March 24, 1998, it settled a lawsuit for copyright infringement filed by Recording Industry Association of America for $9 million. In the historic Class Action suit filed by Boies, Schiller & Flexner, Amway finally surrendered by agreeing to pay over $150 million for settlement before Californian District Court. Besides this the company is compelled to reduce the price of its products.

Amway settled the case in which it was accused for running an illegal pyramid scheme, selling over priced and useless products, violating federal racketeering law, California's "endless chain" law, and the previous ruling against it.

In the year 1986 the US Federal Trade Commission filed two civil penalty complaints, and obtained consent judgement in both. One was for the violation of Commission's order prohibiting deceptive earning claims and this was settled by remitting of a penalty of Rs. $1000000.[2]

US District Court Jury in Salt Lake City directed four of Amway distributors to pay a fine of $ 19.25 million to the Company Proctor and Gamble for spreading false rumours against it.

Canada

Canadian Government sued Amway as early as 1983 as it is found that its IBOs did not have any registration with a government agency to run their business. The charge was for tax evasion as they have obtained neither trade licence from any municipality nor VAT registration. Ultimately, Amway pleaded guilty before the Supreme Court of Ontario and paid a fine of $ 325000000, the largest one ever imposed in Canada.

England

Amway was sued and shut down in England by the Federal regulators for violating England's Fair Trading Act, 1973 and other laws. The Department for Business Enterprise and Regulatory Reform in England held that the Amway scheme is "inherently objectionable", operates as lottery and trading unlawfully. Charge sheet alleged that Amways main activity is to lure others to join the slaes force so that the registration fee can be collected and marketing materials can be sold. The promise of wealth was illusionary and amounted to dream sale.

On 8th November, 2007, Secretary of State for Trade and Industry appealed in the High Court of Justice to wind up Amway in United Kingdom.[3]

In a landmark Judgment the Court pointed out: Amway's products are not marketable. They are priced far higher than comparable goods. They are seldom sold to anyone other than the sales people themselves. More than 99 per cent of all Amway distributors lost money and despite this Amway always misled recruits in England with false income claims. More than half quit the scheme within a year, after suffering financial losses. The only way to make money in Amway is through "endless chain recruiting", a flawed and fraudulent system that guarantees only the top recruiters can be profitable and is illegal in England and most other places on the planet. Extreme deception is used to lure people into the scam.

China

The Government of China has passed a law in 2005 that outlaws the payments of commissions on purchases made by "downline" recruits in the scheme. MLM companies were banned in China. Though, Amway is allowed to operate in China, its pyramid recruitment pay plan is strictly prohibited there.

As there are stretchs of thousands of pages in the internet laying bare the fraudulent nature of Amway's business plan, in the form of various court observations and expert analysis, this is not attempted here. Amway misleads consumers with false income claims and promises for its "business opportunity. Fitz Patrick's *report on the commission payouts of 11 major MLMs* shows that more than 99 per cent of all who sign up with Amway never earn a profit. The website Amway Untold Story is exclusively dedicated for this purpose[4].

Amway everywhere is influencing the politicians who in turn will muzzle regulators. Dick Devos, the son of Amway founder, is married to Betsy Prince, sister of Erik Prince, the founder of Military contracting firm, Blackwater, which wield much political influence in US. Amway and Blackwater are the main contributors to Republican Congress. Consequently Timothy Muris, a lawyer whose firm once represented Amway, was appointed as the Federal Trade Commission's chairman. Muris appointed David Scheffman, who argued for the MLM Company Equinox, as the FTC's new Chief Economist.

India

The response from FICCI, Chamber of Commerce and even the Ministry to the arrest of the Amway MD in India demanding to protect "genuine multilevel marketing companies" shows the need for exposing Amway's business in India. Some argued that no criminality is involved in the Amways business whereas some others argued there is "no clarity in the law" for genuine direct selling. Some even went to the extent of saying that it will give an inappropriate message to the global business community and might also have adverse impact on Indo-US business relationships.

Secretary General, of Indian Direct Selling Association, said, "It is very disappointing and unfortunate that due to lack of clarity between the direct selling business model and fraudulent pyramid schemes, harassment continues. We urge the government to provide clarity immediately." IDSA came forward with their clarifications to the Government on the definitions of the ambiguous schemes." 'Pyramid' is generally associated with direct selling but it is not always the case. We explained what could be Ponzi schemes. But, it is high time that we have a framework like other countries,"[5]

Economic Times written "Fast growing countries such as Thailand, Malaysia, Korea, Indonesia, China, Vietnam, Japan, Taiwan and Singapore all have a specific statute that not only regulates but also facilitates direct selling."

In the wake of all these it is made essential to explain who is lacking clarity in law. It would appear that all the world countries promote the MLM. The argument for protecting Genuine MLM and distinction between pyramid scheme and direct selling etc. are all interesting as these are the arguments raised everywhere when criminal proceedings are initiated against the MLM robbery.

Foreign Investment

Amway Corporation, United States of America, was allowed entry into India by the Foreign Investment Promotion Board in the year 1994 only to develop direct selling business. Consequently Amway Company was registered in Delhi and started functioning since 1996.

As per the information furnished by the Amway Company itself, in the reply to a notice issued by the investigating officer, Amway have conceded that their foreign direct investment up to 2013 is only Rs. 22 crore. Even records with Reserve Bank of India up to 2006 shows that the FDI brought in by the company is Rs. 18 crore. But in an Affidavit claimed by Amway in a writ petition before the Honourable High Court of Andhra Pradesh, it was claimed that it invested Rs. 151 crore in India which is later on proved to be false.

Thus, the decision of the Foreign Investment Promotion Board in giving permission to the Multinational Fraud Company to begin operation in India on the ground for bringing foreign investment has proved to be wrong step as the nominal foreign investment they brought in is only a fraction of the enormous proceeds they earned just within one year of their operation in India.

But, the Balance Sheet filed by Amway for the financial year ending March 2012 shows that revenue earned by Amway from its operation in India during the year was Rs. 2150.41 crore. The net profit, after paying exorbitant commissions to the top leaders and to the extravagant business meets, was Rs. 344.08 crore. Its bank balance for the year was Rs. 373.98 crore. Even after deducting the extravaganza cost, and gains made by senior leaders, the profit earned by Amway as reflected in the balance sheet since 1999 will amount to Rs. 1737.505 crore.

Normally, technology transfer is another ground for allowing foreign collaboration or for foreign direct investment. But, Amway endeavoured to manufacture anything from India and instead they resorted to outsourcing of products.

The company is marketing nearly 300 products. The company does not manufacture any product on its own. The activity of the company is to purchase products from Indian companies, and sell the same through networking at a price of minimum 8 fold of the price at which the manufacturing firm is selling in the retail market.

Even the products imported are not the one manufactured by Amway. The products which can be branded as "lotions, potions and creams" are the ones which do not require any foreign technology as the manufacturing does not involve any technology intensive process.

Table 11.1: List of Contract Manufactures

Sl No.	*Name*	*Place*	*Address*
1.	Sarvotham Care	Baddy	Jharmajri, Baddy, Barotiwala Road, PO Barotiwala, Himachal Pradesh-174103
2.	Naisa Laboratory	Baddy	Village Krishnapura, PO Gurumajra, Baddy, Nalagarh Road, Dist. Solan-174101, Himachal Pradesh
3.	Soft Gel Health Care Pvt. Ltd.	Chennai	Survey No. 20/1 Vandalur-kelembakkam Road. Pupakkam Village. Kanjjepuram Dist. Thamilnadu-603103
4.	Sarvotham Care Ltd.	Hyderabad	1-20-248, Umajay Complex, 2nd Floor, Rasoolpura, Secundarabad-500003
5.	Aura Personal Products	Bhimtal	Khasara No. 1220 to 1224, Plot No. A 3/3 UPSIDC industrial Area, Bhimtal-263136-Utharakhand
6.	Daffy Cosmetics Pvt. Ltd.	Rudrapur	Plot No. 11, Sector-3 SIDCUL, IIE,263, Pantnagar- 263153
7.	VVF (India) Ltd.	Baddi	H.B # 214. V.P.O. Bhatoli Kalan, Dist. Solan, Himachal Pradesh-263153
8.	KLF Nirmal Industries Pvt. Ltd.	Irinjalakkuda	Fr. Dismas Road, PB No. 40, Irinjalakkuda- 680121 Dist. Thrissur, Kerala
9.	Aero Pharma Pvt. Ltd.	Rabele	W-32 TTC Industrial Area, MIDC Village, Rabele, Navi Mumbai-400701
10.	Fiabila India Ltd.	Rabele	V 17, MIDC, Taloja, Dist. Raigad- 410208
11.	Avalon Cosmetics Pvt. Ltd.	Paonta Sahib	158, Dani Compound, CST Road, Kalina, Santacruz (East), Mumbai-400098
12.	JHS Svendgaard Laboratories Limited	Paonta Sahib	Trilokpur Road, Kheri (Kala-amb) Thehsil Nahan, Dist. Sirmour, Himachal Pradesh-173030

Andhra Police sent some of the health products sold by Amway for analysis and report to the Institute of Preventive Medicine, Public Health Lab and Food Administration, Hyderabad and to Drugs Control Administration. The result of examination is surprising. It was found that the products of Amway are not as per standards. Out of 18 health products, 14 are proved to have been misbranded or adulterated. Remaining 4 of them are found not food items by the State Food Laboratory. "Hence, Amway's claim of selling quality products is nothing but an unadulterated falsehood and their scheme evidently amounts to blatant cheating of innocent consumers."[6] Thus, Andhra Police have chargesheeted the company under the provisions of Prevention of Food Adulteration Act, 1954.

Amway Scheme

Amway money circulation scheme is based on the Generation Plan pattern of enrollment of distributors. Sale of products at exorbitant prices coupled with endless chain of intermediaries in between the end consumers and producer makes this a camouflaged money circulation scheme.

The Generation Plan with little variation is adopted by Amway. Basing on a stipulated percentage of margins available from each product incomes are offered to a chain of upline members. Anyone may sponsor as many as possible on their own to make themselves eligible for bonuses.

The commission offered to the members in different layers will be different and it progresses cumulatively, according to the total value of group business, unlike the one in the traditional business where retailer gets the highest percentage of commission.

The chain of intermediaries is grouped together on the basis of the commission structure offered by the company. Contrary to their overt claim of direct selling. Amway awards titles with fancy names to its members depending on number of downline members under each member. Accordingly, the following 22 titles show the chain of intermediaries between the Amway Corporation and the end consumers.

Table 11.2

Sl. No.	*Title*	*Requirements for qualification*
1.	Silver Producer	A silver producer has attained a qualifying month at 21% as defined in the Amway Business Manual
2.	Gold Producer	A gold producer has attained three qualifying months at the Silver Producer Level.

(Contd.)

(Contd.)

Sl. No.	*Title*	*Requirements for Qualification*
3.	Platinum	A platinum has attained six qualifying months at the silver producer level, at least three of which are consecutive.
4.	Ruby	A Ruby is a qualified Platinum who has attained at least 20000 personnel group PV in anyone month during performance year in market.
5.	Founders Platinum	A Founder's Platinum has attained 12 qualifying months at the silver producer level for all months in a performance year.
6.	Founder's Ruby	A Founders' Ruby is qualified Platinum who has maintained 20000 personal group PV for 12 months in a performance year in market.
7.	Sapphire	A Sapphire is a qualified Platinum who has sponsored 2 domestic 21 per cent legs in the same month for 6 months in a performance year whilst maintaining 4000 personnel Group PV or has a third 21 per cent leg in the absence of 4000 GPV in any month.
8.	Founder's Sapphire	A Founder's Sapphire is a qualified Platinum who has sponsored 2 domestic 21 per cent legs in the same month for 12 months in a performance year whilst maintaining 4000 personnel Group PV or has a third 21 per cent leg in the absence of 4000 GPV in any month.
9.	Emerald	A Emerald is a qualified Platinum who has sponsored 3 legs each of which was at the 21 per cent Performance Bonus Level for at least 6 months of the performance year.
10.	Founder's Emerald	A Founder's Emerald is a qualified Platinum who has sponsored 3 legs each of which was

(Contd.)

(Contd.)

Sl. No.	*Title*	*Requirements for qualification*
		at 21 per cent Performance Bonus Level for all the 12 months of the performance year.
11.	Diamond	A Diamond is a Qualified Platinum who has sponsored 6 legs each of which was at 21 per cent performance Bonus Level for at least 6 months of the performance year.
12.	Founder's Diamond	A Founder's Diamond is a qualified Platinum who has sponsored 6 legs each of which was at 21 per cent performance Bonus Level for all the 12 months of the performance year or is a Diamond Bonus recipient who has achieved 8 FAA points.
13.	Executive Diamond	An Executive Diamond is a qualified Platinum who has sponsored 9 legs each of which was at 21 per cent Performance Bonus Level for at least 6 months of the performance year or is a Diamond Bonus recipient who has achieved 10 FAA points.
14.	Founder's Executive Diamond	A Founder's Executive Diamond is a qualified Platinum who has sponsored 9 legs each of which was at 21 per cent Performance Bonus Level for all the 12 months of the performance year or is a Diamond Bonus recipient who has achieved 12 FAA points.
15.	Double Diamond	A Double Diamond is a qualified Platinum who has sponsored 12 legs each of which was at 21 per cent performance Bonus Level for at least 6 months of the performance year or is a Diamond Bonus recipient who has achieved 14 FAA points.

(Contd.)

(Contd.)

Sl. No.	*Title*	*Requirements for qualification*
16.	Founder's Double Diamond	A Founder's Double Diamond is a qualified Platinum who has sponsored 12 legs each of which was at 21 per cent Performance Bonus Level for all the 12 months of the performance year or is a Diamond Bonus recipient who has achieved 16 FAA points.
17.	Triple Diamond	A Triple Diamond is a qualified Platinum who has sponsored 15 legs each of which was at 21 per cent Performance Bonus Level for at least 6 months of the performance year or is a Diamond Bonus recipient who has achieved 18 FAA points.
18.	Founders Triple Diamond	A Founder's Triple Diamond is a qualified Platinum who has sponsored 15 legs each of which was at 21 per cent Performance Bonus Level for all 12 months of the performance year or is a Diamond Bonus recipient who has achieved 20 FAA points.
19.	Crown Diamond	A Crown Diamond is a qualified Platinum who has sponsored 18 legs each of which was at 21 per cent Performance Bonus Level for at least 6 months of the performance year or is a Diamond Bonus recipient who has achieved 22 FAA points.
20.	Founder's Crown	A Founder's Crown is a qualified Platinum who has sponsored 18 legs each of which was at 21 per cent Performance Bonus Level for all 12 months of the performance year or is a Diamond Bonus recipient who has achieved 25 FAA points.
21.	Crown Ambassador	A Crown Ambassador is a qualified Platinum who has sponsored 20 legs each

(Contd.)

(*Contd.*)

Sl. No.	*Title*	*Requirements for qualification*
		of which was at 21 per cent Performance Bonus Level for at least 6 months of the performance year or is a Diamond Bonus recipient who has achieved 27 FAA points.
22.	Founder's Crown Ambassador	A Founder's Crown Ambassador is a qualified Platinum who has sponsored 20 legs each of which was at 21 per cent Performance Bonus Level for all 12 months of the performance year or is a Diamond Bonus recipient who has achieved 30 FAA points.

The above schedule shows that only lip service is paid to the concept of much boasted Direct Selling.

One can join the company free of cost but to continue as a member he should buy products worth at least Rs. 3500 within 60 days of joining. To get incentive one should enroll one person each on either side and incentives increase with the increase in the number of enrollment and the consequent increase in the business volume.

Every product will carry certain volume of points that are counted for the incomes calculations of a distributor. The total of the business value of all the self-purchase and consumer sales made by a distributor together is called self-BV.

TBV: The sum of point value of all the sales happened in a distributor network of a team under a leader is called the team BV. The total of Self BV + Team BV is called Group BV (GBV). Group BV will be a parameter to assign Ranks/designations/which decides percentage of income eligibility.

Every distributor is required to maintain certain self-BV every month to consider as "Active" which alone will give eligibility for income. Thus, every distributor is compelled to make some self-purchase to remain active in the system.

Exorbitant Price

Direct selling envisages eliminating of intermediaries so that the consumers will get the price at the lowest competitive price. But Amway is selling products at 6 to 10 fold of the actual market price as huge amount is required to make payout to different upstair members. Some sales are made to the consumers outside the pyramid at the rate shown as MRP. But this will be an insignificant proportion of the total sale.

The difference in the price at which the product is sold to the new members in the pyramid and that outside pyramid network of distributors will show that the product is sold at almost 10 fold of its actual market price. The investigation in 2013 found the following differences in the price of Amway products:

Table 11.3

Sl. No.	*Item*	*Price*	*MRP*
1.	Alpha Hydroxy Serum Plus	485	2439
2.	Att. Cleanser dry	58	375
3.	Att. Lipstick Choc. Slush	34	275
4.	Att. Toner dry	42	375
5.	Dynamite Shaving foam	66	289
6.	G&H Body Shampoo	51	395
7.	G&H Lotion 250ML	34	395
8.	G&H Lotion 60 ML	13	125
9.	Glister multi-action TP	23	135
10.	Kid Chewable malty vitamin	205	1179
11.	Kids Chewable CFV	230	1519
12.	Kids Chewable Iron	59	659
13.	Kids Chewable Vitamin C	245	1519
14.	Kids Drink mixed fruit	178	969
15.	Leather and Vinyl Sealer	65	310
16.	Nature Show Protein Familypack 1 kg	484	3119
17.	Nature Show Protein powder 200 grms	105	879
18.	Nature Show Protein powder 500 grms	245	1852
19.	Nature Show Protein with Green tea	293	2052

(*Contd.*)

(*Contd.*)

Sl. No.	*Item*	*Price*	*MRP*
20.	Nature show Saw Palmetto & Nettle R	494	2499
21.	Nature show Vision Health Lutien	322	1999
22.	Nature show par selenium ELM	199	1179
23.	Nutrilite Calmag D	61	639
24.	Nutrilite coenzyme Q10	81	1000
25.	Nutrilite Gluecose Health	157	1499
26.	Nutrilite Iron folic-LM	90	779
27.	Personna classic toothbrush	8	84
28.	Personna premium 3 in 1 soap	12	129
29.	Skin Refinishing Lotion	554	2439
30.	TD Night time Cream	589	2479
31.	Time Defiance Day Cream	593	2479
32.	Zoom Conc. 500 ML	46	251
33.	Artistri Lipstic Frosty Hazel	34	275
34.	Artistri Whitening Cream	69	499
35.	Artistri nail inamal	23	142
36.	Attitude foot cream	31	315
37.	Attitude body and hand cream	36	315
38.	Dynamite Shaving Cream	19	90
39.	Dynamite Shaving Foam	65	289
40.	G&H Body Shampoo 60 ML	16	125
41.	Eye Pencil—Topaz Blue	80	350
42.	LOC Multy purpose	78	460
43.	Loose Powder Fair	460	1900
44.	Sat Adv DC Shampoo	65	395
45.	Time Defiance Night Lotion	606	2480
46.	Replenishing Eye Cream	194	800
47.	SA8 Gelzime 1 ltr	187	715
48.	Nature show Kids Drink—Mango	178	970
49.	Attitude Blushers	83	499
50.	Dish Drops 1 L	125	600

No MLM company can work without selling the product at a minimum of 6 fold of the actual market price. The products are sold even at 13 fold of the prices and the above price schedule shows that deposit to the money circulation scheme is hidden in the price of the products.

High prices set by the brand loyalty, governed by the market forces of demand and supply need not be confused with the artificially set high price.

Various incentives and commissions are paid from the price of Amway products like Maximum performance bonus, leadership commission, Ruby commission, monthly depth commission, emerald commission, diamond commission, diamond plus commission, Founders Achievement Award, Founders Distinguished Service Award etc. Besides all these 20 per cent of the price is the company's profit. The leaders are offered tours and travels to distant nations as their stature grows in the hierarchy.

More than 50 per cent of the cost of the goods paid by the end consumers for the Amway product is spent to enrich the top level IBOs.

Open Robbery in the Name of Insurance

Besides product sales Amway had directly cheated thousands of people by looting their hard earned money by running open Pyramid Scheme in the name of Insurance run by its associate companies run by Amsure. The modus is to lure the pubic and prompting them to deposit amount in lakhs in their insurance scheme offering heavy return. The distributors of Amway collected premiums from housewives and other laymen misleading them that they need to remit the installments for three consecutive years and they would be getting double the amount remitted on completing of 3 years. Later on it will be revealed that the term of the insurance policy was for 20 years and not three years.

After making investment they will inform the investor that they will stand by the promise only if the investment is made every year for continuous period of 10 years and that nothing will be returned if the investment is not repeated. Also there is condition to return an amount depending on the profit of the company on their investment portfolio if investment is continued for 3 years. But the return will be only less than 70 per cent of the principal amount stating that they suffered loss in their investment scheme.

In this scheme also members are enrolled under chain recruitment scheme. The senior members are offered good commissions on enrolling new members. The distributors of the Amway Company are canvassing for the policy and the sponsor and persons in the upline get incentive of 60 per cent of the remitted amount.

Besides its own cheating scheme the company is having tie up with Max Life and Royal Sundaram Alliance Insurance Company Ltd. The running of this scheme is in violation of the IRDA directives and guidelines. The company does not have authority to make such public collection.

Amway encourages the existing members to exploit the personal relation to bring their family members, relatives, colleagues and subordinates to enroll into their scheme. Thus, it makes family and neighbourhood as their markethood. Chasing the wild dream of easy money, members influence their kith and kin to enroll as their subordinate and causes irreparable damage to the social fabric.

Whether the business activities being carried on by Amway attract the provisions of Prize Chits and Money Circulation Schemes (Banning) Act, 1978 is considered by the Honourable Supreme Court of India in Appeal Petition on the order of Honourable Andhra Pradesh High Court in W.P. Nos. 20470 and 20471 of 2006: The Honourable Court had clearly stated that the Amway scheme specifically attracts offence under sections 3 to 6 of Price Chits and Money Circulation Scheme Banning Act. No major changes were introduced by the company after these judgments.

The virus of camouflaged money circulation schemes, injected by Amway into Indian Economy leads to continuous outflow of money despite the claim of bringing foreign investment. It is a safe conduit for draining away the income and wealth of the country. The illegitimate fund transfers by the company have to be viewed from the perspective of international capital flight. It is high time that the enforcement agencies are awakened to the stark reality that unless restrained, the company will undermine the very fabric of our economy.

References

1. *Setzer* v. *Amway*, 1985 *Affidavit in Support of Defendants' Objections to Plaintiffs' First Request for Production of Documents.*
2. Civil Action No. 86-1360 District Court of Columbia.
3. Companies Court No.2651 of 2007.
4. *Amway: The Untold Story*
   www.cs.cmu.edu/~dst/Amway/AUS/
5. *Post Amway arrests, industry demands regulations for genuine.* articles.economictimes.indiatimes.com ›
6. Charge Sheet against Amway filed by Andhra Police-XIth MM Court-Hyberabad—CC. No. 8/07 and 12/07.

12
Legal Scenario of Money Circulation Schemes

"No wonder law enforcement has been so confused and inconsistent in this arena. Even so, using this analysis, law enforcement agencies can work within existing laws. Attempting to change the laws is risky, since the MLM lobby (Direct Selling Association) could then influence legislators to pass deceptive "anti-pyramid" laws that are actually favourable to MLM, as they have already done in several states."[1]

In most of the countries laws are enacted against the money circulation schemes before experiencing the ramifications of the product based MLM. Thus, anti-pyramid statutes in many countries are not sufficient to combat the present day fraud. The working mechanism of various cheating tools, team building strategies, and the dynamics of fund flow were not experienced and understood at the time of these legislations.

This has caused serious flaws in the crafting of statutes. Also the penal provisions in the existing statutes are not sufficient to take on the international business conglomerates. The absence of provisions for civil remedial along with criminal prosecutions culminate in letting the culprits enjoying the benefits of crime even after facing repeated criminal proceedings.

As the damages caused by the collapse of fraudulent schemes are fatal and widespread, there are deliberations and legislations against it round the world recently. Stringent enforcement of the existing legislation and filling up the legal gap requires a meticulous analysis of the various forms of the fraud.

IMF and World Bank warned the world countries to be bewaring of the dubious schemes. There are several jurisdictions where MLMs are not yet outlawed. This vacuum provided a forum which led to a proliferation of these schemes. But MLM is outlawed in the legal regime in the developed countries like United States of America, the United Kingdom, France, Germany, Italy, Canada, Japan etc. Countries like Romania, Columbia, Malaysia, Norway, Bulgaria, Nepal, Philippines, South Africa also have stringent enactments with un-ambiguous provisions for taking on the MLM companies. China and Mexico have clear and specific law based on objective norms.

It is notable that most of these countries which have enacted laws against pyramid schemes have had incidences of pyramid schemes related activities in the past.

The schemes were presented to the investors as legal entities. Certificates of registration of the firms were conspicuously displayed in their website to create confidence to investors. This aspect is brought to the investigators by many investors. Con men are very keen in getting the presence of government officials and politician in the functions organized by the companies. This gives assurance that the schemes were operating with the knowledge of the Government.

Law enforcing agencies, the worldover has initiated a system of Quack Watch for identifying and curbing this menace and the economic offence wing is now entrusted with the task of prosecuting the promoters of illegal money circulation schemes, currency trading, debit card forging, plastic money scams, internet based cheating and the like.

Anti-Pyramid Legislation in US

In the United States, regulatory authorities like Federal Trade Commission, Securities and Exchange Commission have initiated much enforcement at the Federal Government level. Still anti-pyramid legislation with concrete and all inclusive provisions were passed by the State governments.

California Endless Chain Statute, California Penal Code section 327 says: "Every person who contrives, prepares, sets up, proposes, operates any endless chain is guilty of a misdemeanour. As used in this section, an 'endless chain' means any scheme for the disposal or distribution of property whereby a participant pays a valuable consideration for the chance to receive compensation for introducing one or more additional persons into participation in the scheme or for the chance to receive compensation when a person introduced by the participant introduces a new participant."[2]

It is very clear that the any scheme based on enrollment of new members by the existing members is a criminal offence under this law. More interestingly enrollment of a single additional person by a member is sufficient to constitute an offence.

Oregon Pyramid Statute defines:"pyramid club" means a sales device whereby a person, upon condition that the person make an investment, is granted a licence or right to solicit or recruit for economic gain one or more additional persons who are also granted such licence or right upon condition of making an investment and who may further perpetuate the chain of persons who are granted such licence or right upon such condition".[3]

Though, there is ambiguity in the statutes, the act provides for prosecution against the MLM schemes and through a series of decisions the courts have upheld a variety of abuses as elements of illegal marketing plans.

Even a cursory reading of the above provisions show that the schemes of the American Companies like Amway, Herbalife etc. constitute an offence as per the law in their own land. However, the judicial forums had been following an unenthusiastic and lackadaisical approach towards enforcement of the anti-pyramid laws in U.S.

But, Federal Trade Commission held that the business and distribution structure of Amway was not an illegal pyramid structure because of certain characteristic features. Following the previous decisions Koscot, Ger-Ro-Mar, Holiday Magic cases FTC laid down that scheme can be interpreted as pyramid scheme only if there is existence of huge entry fee, and coercion for large non-returnable purchase to obtain the right to recruit others. Thus, buy back rule and encouraging of retail sales were devised as the tool for overcoming the clutches of law.

The website of Federal trade commission warns: "Pyramid schemes now come in so many forms that they may be difficult to recognize immediately. However, they all share one overriding characteristic. They promise consumers or investors large profit based primarily on recruiting others to join their programme, not based on profits from any real investment or real sale of goods to the public."[4]

FTC points out that product sales are used for hiding the pyramid structure. It can be identified by two signs.

1. *Inventory Loading*: It is phenomenon whereby the recruits are lured to buy more products than they could sell, even at inflated prices through a system of incentives. The top leaders make gain in terms of various commissions for the 'sale' even when little or no products are moved to the market. But the members in the downline have to spent excessive amounts for the inventory that they accumulate.
2. *Another overt manifestation of the pyramid scheme*: It is the lack of retail sales, i.e. sale to the members outside the network. FTC points out "Many pyramid schemes will claim that their product is selling like hot cakes. However, on closer examination, the sales occur only between people *inside* the pyramid structure or to new recruits joining the structure, not to consumers out in the general public."
   But Federal Trade Commission is wrong in asserting that "MLM are actually selling their product to members of the general public, without requiring these consumers to pay anything extra or to join the MLM system. MLM's may pay commissions to a long string of distributors, but these commissions are paid for real retail sales, not for new recruits."

The nexus between the FTC and MLM Industry is described at length in the book written by John M taylor.[5]

The sum collected by the multinational frauds in the name of starting kit which contains pamphlets of the company is "requiring the consumers to pay extra". The assertion that commissions are paid out for retail sales and not for recruits is not correct as most of the American firms are selling their product at a 10 fold price. Thus the dual stand of US legislation is clear and this may be intended to protect the cross boarder gambling of these business tycoons.

Federal Bureau of Investigation

FBI website says: Pyramid schemes, also referred to as franchise fraud, or chain referral schemes, are marketing and investment frauds in which an individual is offered a distributorship or franchise to market a particular product. The real profit is earned, not by the sale of the product, but by the sale of new distributorships. Emphasis on selling franchises rather than the product eventually leads to a point where the supply of potential investors is exhausted and the pyramid collapses[6].

At the heart of each pyramid scheme there is typically a representation that new participants can recoup their original investments by inducing two or more prospects to make the same investment.

Chinese Law

Even in China where market economy is gradually emerging, the MLM scheme started appearing and they were forced to make new enactment. China has very strong laws against Multi-Level Marketing. Still companies like Usana, Primeria etc. are working covertly there. A series of arrests and confiscation of assets have taken place in China over the last one decade.

Chinese Prohibition of Pyramid Selling Regulations

Article 7, describes the following acts to be pyramid selling acts:

1. an organizer or operator seeks illegal benefits by recruiting personnel, requiring the recruited personnel to recruit other personnel to participate, and calculating and paying remuneration (here and hereinafter including material rewards and other economic benefits) to the recruited personnel on the basis of the number of personnel directly or indirectly recruited by them through rolling recruitment;
2. an organizer or operator seeks illegal benefits by recruiting personnel and requiring the recruited personnel to pay fees, or fees in disguised forms such as order of commodities, as a condition to being qualified for participation or recruiting other personnel to participate; and
3. an organizer or operator seeks illegal benefits by recruiting personnel and requiring the recruited personnel to recruit

other personnel so that an upline-downline relationship is formed, and calculating and paying remunerations to an upline personnel on the basis of the sales performance of his down-line personnel.[7]

Still nearly 24 companies including domestic and foreign ones obtained licence to operate in China in the guise of direct selling. This includes transnational fraudulent firms including Amway, Nuskin, Oriflame, Avon etc.

Australian Law

In the Australian Trade Practices Amendment (Australian Consumer Law) Act (No. 2) 2010, there are clear and transparent norms for banning Multi-Level Marketing in Australia.

The law defines:

(1) A *pyramid scheme* is a scheme with both of the following characteristics:

A. To take part in the scheme, some or all new participants must provide, to another participant or participants in the scheme, either of the following (a *participation payment*):

(i) a financial or non-financial benefit to, or for the benefit of, the other participant or participants;

(ii) a financial or non-financial benefit partly to, or for the benefit of, the other participant or participants and partly to, or for the benefit of, other persons;

B. The participation payments are entirely or substantially induced by the prospect held out to new participants that they will be entitled, in relation to the introduction to the scheme of further new participants, to be provided with either of the following (a *recruitment payment*):

(i) a financial or non-financial benefit to, or for the benefit of, new participants;

(ii) a financial or non-financial benefit partly to, or for the benefit of, new participants and partly to, or for the benefit of, other persons.

(2) A *new participant* includes a person who has applied, or been invited, to participate in the scheme.

(3) A scheme may be a pyramid scheme:

(a) no matter who holds out to new participants the prospect of entitlement to recruitment payments;

(b) no matter who is to make recruitment payments to new participants; and

(c) no matter who is to make introductions to the scheme of further new participants.

(4) A scheme may be a pyramid scheme even if it has any or all of the following characteristics:

A. the participation payments may (or must) be made after the new participants begin to take part in the scheme;

B. Making a participation payment is not the only requirement for taking part in the scheme;

C. The holding out of the prospect of entitlement to recruitment payments does not give any new participant a legally enforceable right; and

D. Arrangements for the scheme are not recorded in writing (Whether entirely or partly).[8]

European Union

Recently, Herbalife was held to be illegal by a European Court. The Belgian Court's observation is a landmark judgment which will affect many other MLMs.

The Court held that Herbalife is not a direct selling company as it could not adduce evidence for proving a base of consumers who buy the products on a retail basis from its "distributors". The sales people themsevles buy thousands of dollars of products in order to receive promised commissions gained from recruiting other "salespeople." The court also found that Herbalife pay plan offers much more reward for recruiting than for retailing.

The common argument of the MLM companies that its salespeople are the "retail customers" is rejected by the Court. Saying that both cannot be true at the same time. Salespeople pay fees, sign legally binding contracts that define them as "contractors," and are offered rewards based on recruiting. Herbalife rewards consumer investors for recruiting other consumer investors and the rewards are based upon an unsustainable and "dishonest" system of endless recruiting.[9]

In New Zealand pyramid schemes are prohibited under the Fair Trading Act and it is enforced by Commerce Commission. It protects the consumers from misleading and deceptive trade practices.[10]

Thus, new enactments are taking part the worldover, precisely defining the Multi-Level Maketing to be pyramid schemes and the well crafted dictums like participation payments and recruitment payments give no room for camouflaging.[11]

References

1. John M Taylor, (2003), *MLM Definitions and Legitimacy*, online book.
2. *MLM Laws in 50 State*, Jeffrey A. Babener, 2010.
3. *Ibid.*
4. Debra A. Valentine, *IMF Seminar on current issues affecting Central Banking*: http://www.ftc.gov/speeches/other/dvimf16.shtm.
5. John M. Taylor (2003), *op.cit.*
6. FBI Common Fraud Schemes: http://www.fbi.gov/majcases/fraud/fraudschemes.htm
7. China Trade in Services: http://tradeinservices.mofcom.gov.cn/en/b/2005-08-23/24294.shtml
8. http://www.comlaw.gov.au/ComLaw/Legislation/Act1.nsf/0/4E8004BC23ACDEBBCA2577620009E209/$file/1032010.pdf
9. Commercial Court in Brussels No. JC-DC/27.
10. Lehman, Lee & Xu, *China Knowledge International Perspective.*
11. Door to Door Selling—Pyramid Selling—Multi-Level Marketing Contract no. a0/7050/98/000156—A Study Commissioned by the European Commission, final report.

13
Major Scams in India

The con artistes have experimented all the different sorts of financial frauds ranging from open pyramid schemes to the most modern intricate and camouflaged swindling schemes.

Open Pyramid Schemes

Stock Guru India

By running an open Pyramid Scheme, Stock Guru India have collected over Rs. 1100 crore, from the investors spread mainly in Metropolitan cities like Delhi and Mumbai, promising to double investors' money in six months. When legal proceedings started, the promoters went to the extent of intimidating the investors by issuing a veiled threat by issuing public notice 'If you file a criminal case against us, then also you need to come in front of the Income Tax department as party, as you will have to make statements in police stations.... That statement will be used to file a case against you in the Income Tax department for evading taxes in case you have not shown the amount in your income tax file."[1]

The MD of the firm warned the investors to reveal the details of payout to senior members to the Income Tax Department and posted in the Net: "Please make the IT department as a party in any of your case, as they have your money and not us. So, make them party to recover your money as.... I have nothing left with me...". When he is arrested; finally, as many as 12 cars and 63 crore rupees in cash were seized, and 94 bank accounts were frozen.

Money Makes Money

By offering 30 per cent monthly return through the website, www.mmmindian.in, the Russian Company, MMM Russia have collected almost Rs. 250 crore from India, without even a registration in India. They appealed gullible public with "Fantastic Plan. Give Help and Get Help... We are going to create a Boom in your City... Day-by-day we are making new records in this dynamic and magic plan." The plan took major Indian cities by storm. The scheme was spread through messages to thousands of email IDs obtained from database of various MLM websites like www.MLMPortal.net etc.... They challenged the enforcement by posting in their Site: *"No Government or no law Can Ban a System Or Policy Or Unit Or Organisation Which Help Each Other ... In Doing Transactions Between each other. So this System is Not Against Any Law In Any Country. MMM is just like NGO, a Non-Governmental Organisation."*

Finally, *nearly* 4 lakh members got enrolled in the scheme within a few months and collections were direct. Earnings of members were shown as e-wallet points. "*no rbi, no income tax, can close this system, its my challenge for all of u my friends. so enjoy benefits till long term. Within 2 years all Indians will become investors of this system, ...helping each other is not a crime...not against law...not against govt...not against rbi....not against income tax ok.*"[2]

Within no time, clones of this model erupted at various parts of the country offering to double the money even in 7 days. MMM too had a tragic end and three Russians were arrested in Mumbai.

Tycoon Empire International

Tycoon Empire International and its associates have swindled away 250 crore of rupees from 1.25 lakh people. For evading tracking in a subsequent stage they were clever to get the company registered with fake address of the directors. Offering fabulous return in the form of Loyalty commission, Spot commission and Enrollment commission, they could create tremors among the crazy investors spread mainly in Kerala and Tamil Nadu. The money receipts in the scheme were recorded as sales proceeds of some unheard products to dupe the investors. But Sale was only symbolic.

There was frequent changing of directorship. The real kingpin, Narayana Narasimhalu, a senior political leader, remained behind the curtain, posing his coolie workers as directors. Mason workers were presented as business management experts who had their education in the US. The wily politician was smart enough to keep himself aloof from the operations of the company as he knew that the entire operation was against the law.

The scheme spread even to the remote villages at a very fast pace. *Senior leaders had gone for aggressive enrollment of new members in their hot pursuit of making quick and easy money and induced the downline members for such enrollment and thereby vigorously promoted the scheme.*

The uneducated directors, who had nothing but the borrowed attire and ostentatious designation, could not attend the pompous business meetings. This made the investors more suspicious. Finally, educated employees in the company were inducted as new directors.

The kingpin behind the company had siphoned off the accumulated fund by transferring it to the bogus accounts of some non-existing entities as though making payments for the purchase made by the company from them. Funds worth crores of rupees were transferred to the account of petty shops, on producing their bills.

Thousands of investors including women from village area lost their hard earned money when the scheme crumbled down. Finally, the leader was arrested and 135 acres of land was attached. All the 10 directors were arrested. A fleet of luxury cars were seized. By that time they designed another con scheme for the sale of land, i.e., the inaccessible, un-demarcated and cheap land in the hilly terrains in the possession of the company was priced several multiples of its purchase cost and was about to sell of it to the members.

Gold Sukh

Gold Sukh Trade India Ltd., another MLM company, swindled nearly Rs. 203 crore from its 1.5 lakh investors. The directors arrested in Gold Sukh case started another company in the name of Aditya Cosmos Pvt. Ltd. and collected Rs. 19 crore from the investors before the second arrest. Gold worth Rs. 2 crore was seized from their office. Three of the directors were again arrested.

Unipay2U

Unipay2U is a Malasian based multinational corporation which minted millions from Indian investors by running pyramid schemes. Best Genius Ltd. was the name of its mother company incorporated in Malasia. Several multilevel marketing companies which spread across the border, mainly in India, Bangladesh, Nepal etc. like Unipay2U, Unigateway2us, Unigold2u and Unipay2U international are the ones run by this company. Unipay2U is incorporated in Chennai with one director from Malaysia and another from India. Unigateway2u has got two Indian directors.

A Jaipur based company, Avanee Trade Link Private Ltd. duped its investors by making an offer of Rs. 4.44 lakh within 11 months if a sum of Rs. 1 lakh is invested by them. Kanak Dhara and BK Jewellery cases of Delhi are also the collective investment scams involving billions.

Eve Miracle is a company which duped 19 thousand investors and the volume of scam is about Rs. 145 crore. Their clients were spread mainly in Maharashtra, Madhya Pradesh and Rajasthan. Finally, investors understood their folly and turned against the company. Its director Shivaji Sharma was arrested finally and 14 kg of gold was seized from the office.

Some of the Indian companies like Visarav extended their operation to Bangladesh which led to the new enactment of law in Bangladesh against MLM companies.

Cheating under the Guise of Product Sales

Ever since 1994 large number of Multi-National Corporation entered into Indian Economy with their dubious schemes of product sales. Amway is the forerunner of these companies and several of their promoters registered their own domestic companies based on their experience with Amway.

Instead of selling goods directly to the end consumers, Amway floated the multi-level marketing scheme of enrolling endless chain of intermediaries as distributors. Thus, in fact Amway is not selling the products direct to the end consumer and there are endless chain of distributors between the producer and the end consumer.

Large number of Indian companies has duplicated the Amway business plan and now-a-days the market is flooded with the sham products of these companies. The consumers are given products at a price of several multiples of their actual market price.

Inway, Goodway, Bamway, Styleway, Primeway etc. are all the companies which devised their own 'ways' for looting the customers. Being the oldest and largest of all the MLM companies, Amway business schemes require a detailed analysis and this will be done in an ensuing chapter separately.

Nano Excel

Nano Excel, a Hyderabad based company, had nearly 40 lakh of customers. Harish Madaneini an MD Doctor had turned into the MLM business seeing the immense scope of accumulation and is now languishing facing hundreds of cases spread all throughout India. The products outsourced from various Indian and Chinese companies are sold at price of 6 to 10 fold of actual market prices. Huge fund is raised through the endless chain recruiting of distributors, paying for some totally unworthy products like Nano Card, Nano Bracelet, Jewel Watch, Tobacco Card, Alcohol Card etc. The products, no units of which can be sold in the open market at the given price rate, are sold rampantly by the company as it is supported by pyramid model enrollment.

RCM

RCM is a 10-year old company which produced 500 products. It followed Growth plan of Multi-Level Marketing. It swindled nearly Rs. 800 crore from Rajasthan through its outlets, named Gold Sukh. It is one of the very big Indian companies with 1.35 crore distributors, paying sales tax Rs. 1.25 crore monthly. Nearly15 lakh cheques were issued by RCM in a month alone. Around 100 branches of various banks operated near the company's head office only for this work.

Following legal action against the company its agents from different places came to Jaipur and Delhi and sat on hunger strike for 85 days. 'Guidelines' were issued by Rajashtan Government in the wake of this strike for 'regulating' the MLM companies.

Some of the standard companies, like Hindustan Lever experimented networking as a method of pushing their popular brands of products. But people rejected the plan as they could get the same products in the open market much below the price offered for the member enrolling the scheme.

Large numbers of foreign firms are working in India with their dubious investment schemes, both as overt pyramid scheme as well as multi-level marketing. Monavie, Nuverus, Skybiz, Gold Quest, Swiss cash, TVI Express, ATCR, Dew soft, RMP,...etc. are all engaged in this mischievous programmes.

Market Survey as a Tool of Deception

Speak Asia Pvt. Ltd., another fraud company which worked through their website **www.SpeakAsiaOnline.com** came with a novel con art of doing marketing survey by an endless chain of online surveyors. The scheme spread like wildfire in India taking away the earnings of large mass of downline members.

The Company claimed it is engaged in the market survey of products by collecting consumer feedback. Anybody can become a surveyor by joining the scheme through an existing member by paying Rs. 12,000 to the company. They will be assigned one survey work in each week with a reward of Rs. 1000 as stipend. Thus, 48 surveys are minimum guaranteed during a year and surveyor can make 48,000 rupees by paying Rs. 12,000. Thus, a return of 400 per cent is offered on investments, in the name of conducting surveys. There was no actual survey and instead forms were simply filled up in fictitious names and forward to the company. Survey was meant only for collecting the entry fee, which is one way of running the pyramid scheme in covert form. Each surveyor has to recruit two others. A payment of Rs. 1000 per pair was offered and thus it was a typical pyramid scheme. Rewards were shown as e-wallet points without any counter balance liquidity with the company.

The plan of chain recruitment of surveyors went on uninterrupted for 15 months. A total of nearly 20 lakh surveyors joined the chain within one year and the volume of Scam was approximately Rs. 2000 crore. Huge funds are transferred to Singapore in a single transaction. Auditor of the Company, who arranged for cross boarder fund transfer, was asked by the court to remit a cash surety equal to the fee he obtained from the company, for granting bail.

Marketing the Antique Value

Quest Net International adopted another method to pursue the money chain business. Company started selling gold coins at an escalated face value claiming it to be a unique antique piece. The chain recruiting business of the company was done for the sale of gold coins and for canvassing customers to its holiday resorts. The company slurged money for organizing flamboyant sports programme with international cricketer as its brand ambassador. The glitterati of Mumbai were swayed by the money madness ignited by Quest Net.

Gradually, the company also met with the fate of other dream merchants. Complaints started pouring in against the company when it could not find more aspiring members.

Q Net is one among the 87 companies which the Ministry of Financial Affairs branded as fraudulent firms.

Land Based Cheating Schemes

Scamsters seeking new avenues for amassment have blended new methodologies of swindling. The notorious criminal Ponzi had new admirers in India, who found that even inaccessible forest land, un-demarcated desert land and under water swamp land can mint money, if marketed using MLM strategy. Collection of deposits issuing bonds and debentures against the security of limited assets and enrollment of promoters offering huge commission has become a new con scheme named Para-banking.

PACL

Pearls Agro-tech Corporation Ltd. (PACL), a Jaipur based company, collected huge deposits from the public under the guise of selling land to the members with the offer of buy back at an escalated price after a few years. The shady operation of the company was exposed by the Madhya Pradesh High Court by observing "Company had been accepting deposits from general public. Admittedly, it had no licence or necessary sanction from the Reserve Bank of India, SEBI or other financial body or it had not followed the mandatory provisions of the Act of 2000. The Petitioner-Company itself stated that on a single day at Gwalior it returned the money of near about 51,000 depositors. It has also filed a list of depositors, which runs into 443 pages. The number of depositors we have not calculated, but, may be 50,000 and it returned the money of near about Rs. 45 crore."[3]

Under installment payment plans, land is allotted after receiving 50 per cent of the value of the plot. Majority of the depositors discontinue the daily or monthly remittance and forget about the invested money at the time of tenure completion. Small amounts of large number of investors are looted in this way.

Fund involving thousands of crores is siphoned off by the company Peerless, the fore-runner of PACL, in the 1980s. Daily income of the poor villagers is collected using uneducated women agents. The agents are paid 35 per cent return. Large number of agents were recruited in allround the country for daily collection. Depositors are turning into agents. There is a hierarchy of 22 levels of commission agents in PACL. The scheme works on the basis of offer of easy money. The payments are contingent on enrollment of more members.

The customer will be in unoccupied physical possession of the plot after execution of registered sale deed. The plot cannot, in any other manner be sold, assigned mortgaged, pledged or alienated without obtaining no dues certificate from the company, till payment of full consideration is made.

In cash down payment plan, land will be allotted in the name of customer after receipt of full consideration. On the completion of tenure, the amount is returned to the customers with 12 per cent interest.

The company claims they are engaged in the business of real estate and the development of agricultural land at various places and organizes the sale of under-developed agricultural land, to prospective buyers and undertakes development of the same. The agreements with the buyers contain several deceptive elements.

Actual deposits raised by the company are several multiples of the market value of the land possessed by the company. Deposits are collected against the security of the value of undivided property. The members from far off states are depositing in the scheme against the barren land in interior places which is not demarcated to the members.

Though the company claims that it owns to an extent of 9043.179 acre in various parts of India, its specific location is not known to the authorities. No piece of land is relinquished in the name of customers. The land in the possession of the company is disproportionate to the number of customers.

Option One

Option One group of industries, consisting of three associate companies based in Calcutta, run their scheme through the domain, www.optiononeindustries.com. The company had gone for collection of public investment against the collateral security of its property, showing an inflated value of Rs. 1000 crore. Collection was mainly through issuing option one debenture. Company paid commission to the marketing people up to 40 per cent of collection. A renowned Music Director was the brand ambassador for this group and payment of Rs. 5 crore to the musician became a scandal.

Property is owned by one company, debentures marketing is done by other company and commissions are paid through yet another company. Legal area of option one website shows the certificate, showing endorsement of ROC for collecting Rs. 1000 crore.

This has become an upcoming trend and following this pattern some other companies also applied for sanction to issue debentures against the value of undivided landed property. Eastern states like West Bengal has become the hub of para banking business and the collection is from Bangladesh also.

Sahara

Sahara the company which is known to the world as the sponsor of high profile sports programmes was engaged in land based collective investment scheme. The company sponsored IPL Cricket team, Pune Warriors, paying Rs. 3.4 crore per test match. It was the main sponsor of Indian cricket team with 42.5 per cent stake in formula 1 Team. Later it withdrew from sponsorship and decided to divert Rs. 500 crore for social work.

The case has become sensational following the ploy resorted to by the company to hoodwink the investigator. In response to the notice to produce documents, they sent two data entry operators to present data which is hosted in US Server. The arrest of its MD, Subrata Roy, prolonged detention and enforcing stringent condition of making remittance to the full extent of liability as surety for the bail is a landmark in the history of prosecution of white collar criminals in India.

When the matter is before the Supreme Court, the company tried the manipulation strategy of filing petition before Allahabad High Court which attracted contempt of court procedure.

Subrata Roy calls himself to be the guardian of nearly one million staff and agents. Finally, Ministry of Corporate Affairs have directed to repay Rs. 23000 crore. The company challenged the SEBI by raising the issue of jurisdiction but the Supreme Court approved the SEBI's stand.

Companies including MPS Greenery Developers, Rose Valley Real Estate and Constructions, Sun-Plant Agro are facing prosecution. SEBI had directed the MPS Greenery Developers to deposit Rs. 1,169.39 crore raised by it in an escrow account with a nationalised bank. The company is restrained from making further collection and from accessing the capital market.

Issuing of Capital Market instruments in the name of agro bonds and plantation bonds by the companies offering exorbitant return, taking advantage of the loopholes of the law could not be cracked down.

Chit Funds

Fraudsters had invented chit funds and *kuris* to be another conduit for public collection draining away the small savings of the large masses. Large numbers of firms are mushrooming in the nook and corner of the country doing the business of chits, without creating any reserve fund or without even a registration in the concerned district and state. Mostly the funds fail after the initial booming and the members find it difficult even to sue these companies as they don't have the basic document of chit agreements. Flouting the provisions of Chit Funds Act, the companies swindle the money of the members.

The fall of Saradha Chits in Bengal opened up a heat of protest by the investors. The activities of the company was shrouded in secrecy and the promoter Sudipto Sen had registered 160 companies. Though the group had done diversified business through large number of firms under an umbrella organization, holding company, ranging from Chit Funds to Real Estate, a staggering amount was collected through Saradha Realty Ltd. Various slabs of investment ranging from Rs. 10,000 to one lakh were collected from the people offering return of 12 to 24 per cent. Besides this there is lump sum investment plan also. Here also money was collected offering to allot land or returns on investment. Collection was several folds of the actual market value of the land possessed by the company.

The company chief was smart enough to dodge the SEBI investigators by resorting to delaying tactics. 230 boxes of documents are submitted as evidence, which are later on found to be irrelevant ones.[4] An estimated Rs. 10,000 crore has been raised by such schemes, says SEBI.

The district court were alleged for supporting the companies by stalling the direction of SEBI by giving injunctions from one district after another.

Of the 86 companies against whom the Ministry of Corporate Affairs (MCA) received complaints for raising un authorized deposits, a whopping 73 were from West Bengal.[5] The bubble of high interest has burst and the government has created a fund of Rs. 500 crore for refunding the depositors.

Emu, Goat Farm, Teak Wood

The investors are allowed to hatch a dream of multiplying their investment in goat farm as goats proliferate into threefold in 6 months. Glossed up advertisement came in full sheet of the newspapers with the stories of how goats are nurtured. Investors are caught up in the story of MS Guru who promised astronomical returns on investment in his firm Susi Emu Farms at Perundurai, near Erode, in Tamil Nadu.

With the huge success of Susi Emu more than 100 companies came up at Perundurai in Erode and neighbouring Tirupur. 'Emu bubble' burst in August 2012, and investors realized that emu farming was a scam only. Hundreds of investors lost their deposited amount as all these firms crumbled down.[6]

Thus all sorts of fraudulent schemes ranging from pyramid schemes, MLM and extortion in the name of chits are rampant in India also. The resultant aftermath is the draining of Indian Capital Market and the regulators including SEBI, RBI, Police and other agencies could not regulate the scam. None of the companies were registered with SEBI despite Collective Investment Scheme Regulations notified in the year 1999.

Funds raised through illegal money circulation scheme are generally flushed to the foreign exchange trading. Currency trading and *hawala* transfers of funds are relying on the funds raised through money circulation schemes. Trading on currency by making advantage of the fluctuations in the international value of currency is another avenue of rotten games. Dubai and Middle East is acting as the hub of international *hawala* operation and currency trading. Liberty reserve, gold cash, alert pay are all companies specializing in Currency trading.

SEBI had initiated legal action against almost 550 entities which float funds. Even when Collective Investment Schemes are dealt with like this, the responsibility of acting against MLM, Pyramid Schemes, and chit fund operators are with State governments. There is need for a single agency to oversee the investment scams. However, this is difficult to materialize as the enforcement is the jurisdiction of the State government. There is need for rationalizing and coordinating the work of various agencies working in the area.[7]

International Organisation of Securities Commissions, a global body of securities market regulators, mooted stronger principles for regulating the collective investment scheme, to safeguard the interest of investors. India welcomed these guidelines amid rising instances of public being defrauded by fraudulent money pooling activities.[8]

Alarmed by the fall of Saradha, Tycoon, Sahara and so on one by one, investors turned anxious about their money and are swarming the offices of these companies across the country. Collapse of these companies has resulted in the customers frenzying for redemption of their invested amounts creating pressure to the existing companies. Promoters are frantically exploring ways to allay public fears.

Panic run on the companies for premature withdrawal posed serious liquidity crunch to the existing companies like Rose Valley, MPS Greenery, iCore E-Services and Tower Info Tech. Many of the company offices were under virtual siege of the distressed investors. It is customary on the part of the companies to give full column advertisements in Newspapers, defining themselves as asset-based companies and not Money Circulation Scheme or 'chit funds'.

Behind the curtain, the illegitimate activities and the swindling is going on uninterrupted in India and is haunting the Indian Capital Market. Large number of websites are still running the con game.

References

1. 'If you go to cops, IT dept will stalk you': posted in the blog Crime Line-by Mateen Hafeez.
2. http://mmmindiask.blogspot.in/2012/12/earn-30-monthly-for-life-time-to_8772.html
3. High Court of Madhya Pradesh-Bench at Gwalior, in Writ Petition No. 3599/2011-between PACL India Ltd. *vs.* State of Madhya Pradesh and others.
4. *Economic Times*, 26.4.13.
5. Con games, Indrani Dutta *The Hindu* Sunday Story 28.4.13.
6. *Ibid.*
7. SEBI Chief UK Sinha in the India Investment Conference.
8. *The Hindu*, April 24, 2013.

14
MLM Against the Backdrop of Indian Law

The evolution of regulatory structure in India is the aftermath of several scams that burnt the fingers of the regulators. Every scam brought in a law; the law is the edifice built on scams and not on intuition.

Money circulation schemes were banned by law in 1978, after Sanchayika Investments went down with money pooled from a few lakh investors in West Bengal. Soon after, chit funds became a hot political issue, leading to a chit fund law in 1982.

Companies are being registered in fake identity and there is no mechanism for checking whether the activities of the companies go beyond the provisions of their memorandum and articles of association. Banks are silent spectators when thousands of crores are collected through accounts of the companies in bogus identity, violating the directives of the Reserve Bank and legal provisions.

There is urgent need for a strengthening regulatory mechanism for tracing these schemes at an early stage and to nip them in the bud. In the wake of an alarming increase in such schemes recently, various State governments have issued various guidelines. In the month of May 2012, State of Manipur issued an alert to the general public regarding such schemes. In July 2011, the High Court of Madhya Pradesh directed the CBI to conduct preliminary enquiry in relation to 33 companies suspected to be violating 'Prize Chits & Money Circulation Scheme (Banning) Act, 1978'.

The power of making rule is vested with the State governments in the Prize Chits & Money Circulation Schemes (Banning) Act, 1978. The State Governments are to frame Rules in consultation with the Reserve Bank of India (RBI). The job of ensuring consistency in making such rules would lie with the RBI.

As the schemes originated in one state will virally spread nation-wide within a short period this can be controlled better at a national level by the Central agencies. MLM companies are making use of this regulatory gap for running their unethical and illegal pyramidal marketing schemes, exploiting this situation.

Companies are operating from abroad even without registration in India. Serious Fraud Investigation Office under the Ministry of Corporate Affairs is established to combat these offences. In one of the judgment of Andhra Pradesh High Court, it has been held that the police have the power to seal the office premises. But as State Governments normally operate within their own jurisdiction, the company continues to operate in the rest of the country with high profile advertisement campaigns on the national television channels. All these call forth a uniform and consistent Central rule for combating this menace.

PRIZE CHITS AND MONEY CIRCULATION SCHEME (BANNING) ACT, 1978

Unlike several countries which had the anti-money circulation scheme legislations in the recent past only, we have enacted the Prize Chits and Money Circulation Scheme (Banning) Act, long back in 1978. Though un regulated investment schemes were not so rampant during 70s, the Act contains clear provisions for prosecuting the offenders.

Section 2(c) defines Money Circulation Scheme as a "any scheme by whatever name called, for making quick or easy money or for the receipt of any money or valuable thing as the consideration for a promise to pay money on an event of contingency relative or applicable to the enrollment of members into the scheme, whether or not such money or thing is derived from the entrance money of the members of such scheme or periodical subscriptions."

Section 3 of the PCMC Act provides that no person shall promote or conduct any Money Circulation Scheme or prize chit or shall enroll as a member in such scheme or participate in it. Thus, promoting such scheme and even simply joining such scheme is defined as a criminal offence punishable with 3 years of rigorous imprisonment and a fine of Rs. 5,000.

RESERVE BANK OF INDIA ACT

It is quite embarrassing to see that Banking Sector which will be worst affected by these schemes are unknowingly conniving the offence. The lukewarm approach of the banks to enforce directives of the Apex Bank on bulk transaction monitoring and bank authorities becoming stooge of some unholy dignitaries are all noticed despite clear and specific provisions in the RBI Act.

The companies running pyramid schemes are collecting money through its accounts in various banks. Banks remain silent spectators when crores of funds are accumulated in the accounts opened in the name of directors in bogus address. Likewise payout to the senior leaders are made through their bank accounts. Even when criminal investigation is started the authorities help the culprits in withdrawing huge funds using fake vendor bill violating the provisions of PML Act. Enforcement of existing Act and rules is sufficient to bring the operation of these companies under stranglehold. Sheer negligence is noticed from the side of the banks in enforcing the provisions for preventing money laundering.

The Act contains several provisions which can be effectively enforced against the companies running collective investment schemes. The compulsion for obtaining registration certificate from RBI, provision for constituting reserve fund for protecting the interest of the depositors, provision against malicious advertisement, provision for freezing the assets of the companies obtained using proceeds of crime are all the tools in the hands of the regulators for fighting the menace of pyramid and MLM schemes.

Registration Certificate from RBI

The Act makes it mandatory for the companies to obtain a Certificate of Registration from the RBI before commencing of business after complying a extensive norms.

Section 45-I A of RBI Act provides that no non-banking financial company shall commence or carry on the business of a non-banking financial institution without–

(a) Obtaining a certificate of registration issued under RBI Act.

(b) having the net owned fund of twenty-five lakh rupees or such other amount, not exceeding two hundred lakh rupees, as the Bank may, by notification in the Official Gazette, specify.

No NBFI can work without applying for registration to the RBI in specified form and such applications will be considered only on fulfilling the following conditions:

(a) that the non-banking financial company is or shall be in a position to pay its present or future depositors in full as and when their claims accrue;
(b) that the affairs of the non-banking financial company are not being or are not likely to be conducted in a manner detrimental to the interest of its present or future depositors;
(c) that the general character of the management or the proposed management of the non-banking financial company shall not be prejudicial to the public interest or the interest of its depositors;
(d) that the non-banking financial company has adequate capital structure and earning prospects;
(e) that the public interest shall be served by the grant of certificate of registration to the non-banking financial company to commence or to carry on the business in India;
(f) that the grant of certificate of registration shall not be prejudicial to the operation and consolidation of the financial sector consistent with monetary stability, economic growth and considering such other relevant factors which the Bank may, by notification in the Official Gazette, specify; and
(g) any other condition, in the interest of the public or depositors.

The above conditions make it clear that no shell company, i.e. those which are neither engaged in manufacturing or providing services or the one without any solid asset base can carry on the business of fund collection.

Even the certificate of registrations granted by the RBI under section 45(5) can be cancelled if such company:

(i) Ceases to carry on the business of a non-banking financial institution in India; or
(ii) has failed to comply with any condition subject to which the certificate of registration had been issued to it; or
(iii) at any time fails to fulfil any of the conditions referred to in clauses (a) to (g) of sub-section (4); or
(iv) fails (a) to comply with any direction issued by the Bank under the provisions of the Act or (b) to maintain accounts in accordance with the requirements of any law or any direction or order issued by the Bank under the provisions of this Chapter; or (c) to submit or offer for inspection its books of account and other relevant documents when so demanded by an inspecting authority of the Bank; or

Reserve Fund

For ensuring liquidity to the non-banking financial companies section 45-IC of the Act provides for a Reserve Fund and make it mandatory to transfer therein a sum not less than twenty per cent of its net profit every year. No appropriation of any sum from the Reserve Fund shall be made by the non-banking financial company except for the purpose as may be specified by the Bank from time to time and every such appropriation shall be reported to the Bank within twenty-one days from the date of such withdrawal.

When the pyramid schemes collapse due to liquidity crunch and millions of downline members are destined to forgo their deposited amount. If the provision for maintaining reserve fund is strongly insisted the members could have claimed this.

Prohibition on Advertisement

Section 45J of the Act authorizes the RBI to regulate or prohibit issue of prospectus or advertisement soliciting deposits of money. In the public interest the Bank may, by general or special order,

(a) Regulate or prohibit the issue by any non-banking institution of any prospectus or advertisement soliciting deposits of money from the public; and
(b) Specify the conditions subject to which any such prospectus or advertisement, if not prohibited, may be issued.

The prospectus of listed companies offering fabulous return can be prohibited invoking this section. There are several instances of the companies giving misleading advertisements even when investigation is commenced against them.

Prohibition on Alienation of Assets

Section 45 MB confers power to the RBI to prohibit the non-banking financial company from accepting any deposit on violation of any of the condition in the Act and can direct, the non-banking financial company against which an order prohibiting from accepting deposit has been issued, not to sell, transfer, create charge or mortgage or deal in any manner with its property and assets without prior written permission of the Bank.

Prohibition on Accepting Deposits

Section 45 S of the Act says that:

(1) No person, being an individual or a firm or an unincorporated association of individuals shall, accept any deposit–
  (i) If his or its business wholly or partly includes any of the activities specified in clause (c) of section 45-I; or
  (ii) If his or its principal business is that of receiving of deposits under any scheme or arrangement or in any other manner, or lending in any manner;

Thus, RBI Act provides several regulatory tools for controlling the companies, the strict invoking of which will strengthen the regulatory mechanism against the unholy and tainted activities of para banking industries in the country.

Know Your Customer

In exercising the powers conferred on it under the RBI Act the RBI has issued several guidelines through which strict norms are set forth for ensuring ongoing monitoring of funds as KYC procedures, i.e. 'Know Your Customer'. The following basic guidelines are issued by the Bank as early as 2004.[1]

Customer Acceptance Policy (CAP)

The customers are to be accepted by Banks on the basis of some explicit criteria. The Customer Acceptance Policy envisages the implementation of following norms:

(i) No account is opened in anonymous or fictitious/benami name(s);

(ii) Customers are to be classified on the basis of the perceptive risks. This will depend on the nature of business activity of the customer, location of customer and his clients, mode of payments, volume of turnover, social and financial status etc.

(iii) Documentation requirements and other information to be collected in respect of different categories of customers depending on perceived risk. This should also follow the requirements of PML Act, 2002 and RBI guidelines.

(iv) Accounts are not to be opened or closed when the bank is unable to verify the identity. It cannot do so when documents required as per the risk categorization could not be obtained due to non-cooperation of the customer or when information furnished is not reliable.

(v) Circumstances, in which a customer is permitted to act on behalf of another person/entity, should be clearly spelt out in conformity with the established law and practice of banking. There could be occasions when an account is operated by a mandate holder or where an account may be opened by an intermediary in the fiduciary capacity. Customers' identity are to be checked for knowing whether they have any criminal background or whether they belongs to any banned entities such as individual terrorists or terrorist organizations etc.

Customer Identification Procedure (CIP)

There has to be a customer identification procedure for carrying out at different stages, i.e. while establishing a banking relationship; carrying out a financial transaction or when the bank has a doubt about the authenticity of the previously obtained customer identification data.

Customer's identity can be verified by relying on independent source documents or information. Sufficient information need be collected for establishing the identity of each new customer. The bank must be able to satisfy the competent authorities that due diligence was observed based on the risk profile of the customer. Such risk based approach is considered necessary to avoid disproportionate cost to banks and a burdensome regime for the customers.

Besides risk perception, the nature of information/documents required would also depend on the type of customer (individual, corporate etc.). For customers that are natural persons, the banks should obtain sufficient identification data to verify the identity of the customer, his address/location, and also his recent photograph. For customers that are legal persons or entities, the bank should (i) verify the legal status of the legal person/entity through proper and relevant documents, (ii) verify that any person purporting to act on behalf of the legal person/entity is so authorized and identify and verify the identity of that person, and (iii) understand the ownership and control structure of the customer and determine who are the natural persons who ultimately control the legal person.

Banks may, however, frame their own internal guidelines based on their experience, normal bankers' prudence and the legal requirements. The bank should take reasonable measures to identify the beneficiaries and should verify their identity.

Monitoring of Transactions

Ongoing monitoring is an essential element of effective KYC procedures. Banks can effectively control and reduce their risk only if they have an understanding of the normal and reasonable activity of the customer. Then the banks can identify transactions that fall outside the regular pattern of activity.

All unusually large transactions and those with no visible economic or lawful purpose are to catch the special attention of the banks. Particular category of accounts may be assigned threshold limits.

High-risk accounts are to be subjected to intensive monitoring. Transactions that involve large amounts of cash inconsistent with the normal and expected activity of the customer should particularly attract the attention of the bank. Very high account turnover inconsistent with the size of the balance maintained may indicate that funds are being 'washed' through the account.

Every bank should set key indicators for such accounts, taking note of the background of the customer, such as the country of origin, sources of funds, the type of transactions involved and other risk factors. Banks should put in place a system of periodical review of risk categorization of accounts and the need for applying enhanced due diligence measures.

Banks should ensure that a record of transactions in the accounts is preserved and maintained as required in terms of section 12 of the PML Act, 2002. It may also be ensured that transactions of suspicious nature and/or any other type of transaction notified under section 12 of the PML Act, 2002, is reported to the appropriate law enforcement authority.

Banks should ensure that its branches continue to maintain proper record of all cash transactions of Rs. 5 lakh and above. The internal monitoring system should have an inbuilt procedure for reporting of such transactions and those of suspicious nature to controlling/head office on a fortnightly basis.

Risk Management

The Board of Directors of the bank should ensure that an effective KYC programme is put in place by establishing appropriate procedures and ensuring their effective implementation. It should cover proper management oversight, systems and controls, segregation of duties, training and other related matters. Responsibility should be explicitly allocated within the bank for ensuring that the bank's policies and procedures are implemented effectively. Banks may, in consultation with their boards, devise procedures for creating Risk Profiles of their existing and new customers and apply various Anti Money Laundering measures keeping in view the risks involved in a transaction, account or banking/business relationship.

Banks' internal audit and compliance functions have an important role in evaluating and ensuring adherence to the KYC policies and procedures. As a general rule, the compliance function should provide an independent evaluation of the bank's own policies and procedures, including legal and regulatory requirements. Banks should ensure that their audit machinery is staffed adequately with individuals who are well-versed in such policies and procedures. Concurrent/Internal Auditors should specifically check and verify the application of KYC procedures at the branches and comment on the lapses observed in this regard. The compliance in this regard may be put up before the Audit Committee of the Board on quarterly intervals.

Banks must have an ongoing employee-training programme so that the members of the staff are adequately trained in KYC procedures. Training requirements should have different focuses for frontline staff, compliance staff and staff dealing with new customers. It is crucial that all those concerned fully understand the rationale behind the KYC policies and implement them consistently.

Customer Education

Implementation of KYC procedures requires banks to demand certain information from customers which may be of personal nature or which has hitherto never been called for. This can sometimes lead to a lot of questioning by the customer as to the motive and purpose of collecting such information. There is, therefore, a need for banks to prepare specific literature/pamphlets etc. so as to educate the customer of the objectives of the KYC programme. The front desk staff needs to be specially trained to handle such situations while dealing with customers.

RBI had Directed the Banks Through to Keep a Sharp Eye on the Money Laundering Through Its Directives[1]

"Transactions that involve large amounts of cash inconsistent with the normal and expected activity of the customer should particularly attract the attention of the bank. Very high account turnover inconsistent with the size of the balance maintained may indicate that funds are being 'washed' through the account.

Banks should ensure that a record of transactions in the accounts is preserved and maintained as required in terms of section 12 of the PML Act, 2002. It may also be ensured that transactions of suspicious nature and/or any other type of transaction notified under section 12 of the PML Act, 2002, is reported to the appropriate law enforcement authority.

Banks should ensure that its branches continue to maintain proper record of all cash transactions (deposits and withdrawals) of Rs. 10 lakh and above. The internal monitoring system should have an inbuilt procedure for reporting of such transactions and those of suspicious nature to controlling/head office on a fortnightly basis."[2]

Withdrawing of funds involving hundreds of crores of rupees as part of siphoning off the funds, by transferring the same to the bogus accounts of non-existent entities, on production of vendor bill from such shops could be done by the Money Chain and MLM companies sheerly out of the negligence of the bankers in scrupulously following the above guidelines.

Even collection of Funds by the MLM companies using bank accounts were brought to the specific notice of the bankers in the country through its directive.[3]

These 'Know Your Customer' guidelines have been revisited in the context of the Recommendations made by the Financial Action Task Force (FATF) on Anti-Money Laundering (AML) standards and on Combating Financing of Terrorism (CFT). These standards have become the international benchmark for framing Anti-Money Laundering and Combating Financing of Terrorism policies by the regulatory authorities

Banks should continue to ensure that any remittance of funds by way of demand draft, mail/telegraphic transfer or any other mode and issue of travellers' cheques for value of Rupees fifty thousand

and above is effected by debit to the customer's account or against cheques and not against cash payment.

Banks should ensure that the provisions of Foreign Contribution and Regulation Act, 1976 wherever applicable are adhered to strictly.

These guidelines are issued under Section 35A of the Banking Regulation Act, 1949 (AACS) and any contravention of or non-compliance with the same may attract penalties under the relevant provisions of the Act.

After mentioning the name of some of the MLM Companies, RBI have pointed out that the incidents of mobilizing large amounts of deposits from unsuspecting public with promise of high returns has come to their notice. It warned the banks that MLM companies open accounts at various bank branches and deposits are collected from different parts of the country through those accounts. RBI has urged banks to be extremely careful before issuing large number of cheque books to these firms.

"The firms and their agents had reportedly promised very high returns on deposits and lured common people to part with funds in the name of certain investment/deposit schemes. These funds, running into crores of rupees, were being pooled at the Principal Accounts of the MLM firms and the funds were eventually flowing out of those Principal Accounts for purposes apparently illegal or highly risky. These firms had managed to get very large number of cheque books issued from the banks and they have, in turn, issued to the depositors, post-dated cheques for small amounts representing future interest dues and deposit payments. The small depositors were depositing the money in the accounts of MLMs at places far away from the places where the accounts were actually opened which was facilitated by Core Banking Solution (CBS) offered by the banks."

The firms are engaged in taking deposit involving unusually high returns. Repayments of interest and deposit amounts in respect of existing deposits would depend on continuous and uninterrupted flow of fresh deposits with increasing volumes. At some stage, the flow of deposits is bound to be stifled. Post-dated cheques tendered thereafter would bounce, due to inadequate funds available in the accounts.

Even the details of some domains advertising their deposit schemes were widely circulated.

"Preliminary reports reveal that the names of the banks, where the MLM firms or their agents were maintaining accounts were getting associated with such operations of MLM firms. This has potential reputational risk for the banks, especially in the event of the firms failing to repay the depositors. Incidentally, as it appears, during personal contacts with the prospective depositors some of these MLM firms or their agents had used the name of the banks where they had accounts."

In view of the above, the RBI advised the banks to be careful in opening accounts of the marketing/trading agencies etc. UBD.PCB. Cir. 30/09.161.00/2004-05 dated December 15, 2004, strict compliance with KYC and AML guidelines issued by RBI was again reiterated.

"In cases where accounts have already been opened in the names of the marketing agencies, retail traders, investment firms, the banks may undertake quick reviews. Wherever large number of cheque books has been issued to such firms, the relative decision may be reviewed in the light of the following:

- Whether the cheque books have been issued to customers on the basis of their express request and after following the internal processes laid down in the matter.
- Whether the number of cheque books is consistent with/ matching the profile of the customers as also their nature of business operations.

Even where the volume of transactions/profile of the customers apparently justify the number of cheque books issued, special ongoing monitoring of the operations in the accounts of such types of firms should be made especially if large volumes of small cash deposits are being made in those accounts and withdrawals are being made therefrom, through cheques written for small amounts, either across the counters or through clearing. In respect of such account holders banks may, in specific cases, call for the data from the account holders on the number and aggregate amount of post-dated cheques issued. The data/information so collected should be analysed in select cases to rule out the possibility of the firms being engaged in deposit taking activities.

Certain indicative parameters for selecting accounts for further scrutiny and action are the bunching of dates of the post-dated cheques, the uniformity in the amounts of cheques etc. These data should be analysed together with data on cash deposits of small amounts on previous distant dates resembling the deposit contracting/ mobilizations dates in terms of similar bunching and uniformity of amounts."

The Apex Bank had given clear direction to report, in case any unusual operations are noticed during review, to the RBI as well as to the Financial Intelligence Unit, Department of Revenue, Ministry of Finance, Government of India.

Despite this much of clear and specific directives thousands of companies running money circulations scheme are floating funds through the banks and this goes on uninterrupted. This calls forth strict prosecution steps against the bankers for the violations on their side.

SECURITIES AND EXCHANGE BOARD OF INDIA ACT

The Securities and Exchange Board of India Act is formulated to control the securities market and it imposes several restraints on the activities of dubious firms.

Protecting the interest of investors in securities and regulating the securities market is the duty of the SEBI.

(2) confers authority for regulating the business in stock exchanges and any other securities markets. SEBI can regulate the stock brokers, share transfer agents, bankers, trusts, merchant bankers, portfolio managers, investment advisers and such other intermediaries who may be associated with securities markets.

The working of venture capital funds and collective investment schemes including mutual funds are under the regulatory framework of SEBI. Money Circulation Scheme comes within the purview of Collective Investment Scheme. Prohibiting of fraudulent and unfair trade practices relating to securities markets are also the responsibilities. It can call for information and record from any bank or any other firms to regulate or prohibit issue of prospectus, or advertisement soliciting money for issue of securities.

Section 11A (1) of SEBI Act says that the Board may, for the protection of investors,

(a) specify, by regulations (i) the matters relating to issue of capital, transfer of securities and other matters incidental thereto; and (ii) the manner in which such matters shall be disclosed by the companies;
(b) by general or special orders (i) prohibit any company from issuing prospectus, any offer document, or advertisement soliciting money from the public for the issue of securities; and (ii) specify the conditions subject to which the prospectus, such offer document or advertisement, if not prohibited, may be issued.

Collective Investment Scheme

11AA. (1) Any scheme or arrangement which satisfies the conditions referred to in sub-section (2) shall be a collective investment scheme.

The board may, for the protection of investors, specify, by regulations, any scheme or arrangement made or offered by any companies in relation to matters of issue of capital, transfer of securities and other matters incidental thereto:

(i) the contributions, or payments made by the investors, by whatever name called, are pooled and utilized solely for the purposes of the scheme or arrangement;
(ii) the contributions or payments are made to such scheme or arrangement by the investors with a view to receive profits, income, produce or property, whether movable or immovable from such scheme or arrangement;
(iii) the property, contribution or investment forming part of scheme or arrangement, whether identifiable or not, is managed on behalf of the investors;
(iv) the investors do not have day-to-day control over the management and operation of the scheme or arrangement.

MONEY LAUNDERING ACT

Section 3 of the Prevention of Money Laundering Act, 2002 defines offence of money laundering as: Whosoever directly or indirectly attempts to indulge or knowingly assists or knowingly is a party or is actually involved in any process or activity connected with the proceeds of crime and projecting it as untainted property shall be guilty of offence of money laundering. Section 4 of the Act specifies the penalty.

Obligations of NBFCs in Terms of Rules Notified Thereunder

NBFCs were advised to appoint a Principal Officer and put in place a system of internal reporting of suspicious transactions and cash transactions of Rs. 10 lakh and above. In this connection, Government of India, Ministry of Finance, Department of Revenue, issued a notification dated July 1, 2005 in the Gazette of India, notifying the Rules under the Prevention of Money Laundering Act (PMLA), 2002.

Section 12 of the PMLA, 2002 casts certain obligations on the NBFCs in regard to preservation and reporting of customer account information. NBFCs are, therefore, advised to go through the provisions of PMLA, 2002 and the Rules notified thereunder and take all steps considered necessary to ensure compliance with the requirements of section 12 of the Act. NBFCs should introduce a system of maintaining proper record of all cash transactions of the value of more than rupees ten lakh. All series of cash transactions integrally connected to each other which have been valued below rupees ten lakh where such series of transactions have taken place within a month and the aggregate value of such transactions exceeds rupees ten lakh; all suspicious transactions whether or not made in cash.

NBFCs are required to maintain information in respect of (i) the nature of the transactions; (ii) the amount of the transaction and the currency in which it was denominated; (iii) the date on which the transaction was conducted; and (iv) the parties to the transaction.

NBFCs should take appropriate steps to evolve a system for proper maintenance and preservation of account information in a manner that allows data to be retrieved easily and quickly whenever required or when requested by the competent authorities. Further, NBFCs should maintain for at least ten years from the date of cessation of transaction between the NBFCs and the client, all necessary records of transactions, both domestic or international, which will permit reconstruction of individual transactions (including the amounts and types of currency involved, if any) so as to provide, if necessary, evidence for prosecution of persons involved in criminal activity.

NBFCs should ensure that records pertaining to the identification of the customer and his address (e.g. copies of documents like passports, identity cards, driving licences, PAN, utility bills etc.) obtained while opening the account and during the course of business relationship, are properly preserved for at least ten years after the business relationship is ended. The identification records and transaction data should be made available to the competent authorities upon request.

Reporting to Financial Intelligence Unit of India

It is advised that in terms of the PMLA Rules, NBFCs are required to report information relating to cash and suspicious transactions to the Director, Financial Intelligence Unit-India (FIU-IND)

(I) NBFCs should carefully go through all the reporting formats. There are altogether five reporting formats prescribed for a banking company, *viz.* (i) Manual reporting of cash transactions, (ii) Manual reporting of suspicious transactions, (iii) Consolidated reporting of cash transactions by Principal Officer of the bank, (iv) Electronic data structure for cash transaction reporting, and (v) Electronic data structure for suspicious transaction reporting which are enclosed to this circular. The reporting formats contain detailed guidelines on the compilation and manner/procedure of submission of the reports to FIU-IND. *NBFCs are advised to adopt the format prescribed for banks with suitable modifications. It would be necessary for NBFCs to initiate urgent steps to ensure electronic filing of cash transaction report (CTR) as early as possible*. The related hardware and technical requirement for preparing reports in an electronic format, the related data files and data structures thereof are furnished in the instructions part of the concerned formats. However, NBFCs which are not in a position to immediately file electronic reports may file manual reports to FIU-IND. While detailed instructions for filing all types of reports are given in the instructions part of the related formats, NBFCs should scrupulously adhere to the following:

(a) The cash transaction report (CTR) for each month should be submitted to FIU-IND by 15th of the succeeding month. While filing CTR, individual transactions below rupees fifty thousand may not be included;
(b) The Suspicious Transaction Report (STR) should be furnished within 7 days of arriving at a conclusion that any transaction, whether cash or non-cash, or a series of transactions integrally connected are of suspicious nature. The Principal Officer should record his reasons for treating any transaction or a series of transactions as suspicious. It should be ensured that there is no undue delay in arriving at such a conclusion once a suspicious transaction report is received from a branch or any other office. Such report should be made available to the competent authorities on request;
(c) The Principal Officer will be responsible for timely submission of CTR and STR to FIU-IND;
(d) Utmost confidentiality should be maintained in filing of CTR and STR with FIU-IND. The reports may be transmitted by speed/registered post, fax, email at the notified address;
(e) It should be ensured that the reports for all the branches are filed in one mode, i.e. electronic or manual; and
(f) A summary of cash transaction report for the NBFC as a whole may be compiled by the Principal Officer of the NBFC in physical form as per the format specified. The summary should be signed by the Principal Officer and submitted both for manual and electronic reporting.

NBFCs may not put any restrictions on operations in the accounts where an STR has been made. However, it should be ensured that there is no tipping off to the customer at any level.

These instructions are issued under Sections 45K and 45L of the Reserve Bank of India Act, 1934 and Rule 7 of Prevention of Money-laundering (Maintenance of Records of the Nature and Value of

Transactions, the Procedure and Manner of Maintaining and Time for Furnishing Information and Verification and Maintenance of Records of the Identity of the Clients of the Banking Companies, Financial Institutions and Intermediaries) Rules, 2005. Any contravention thereof or non-compliance shall attract penalties.

In terms of instructions contained in the guidelines on 'Know Your Customer Norms' and 'Anti-Money Laundering Measures', NBFCs are required to prepare a profile for each customer based on risk categorization. Further, the need for periodical review of risk categorization has been emphasized.

NBFCs are required to put in place an appropriate software application to throw alerts when the transactions are inconsistent with risk categorization and updated profile of customers. It is needless to add that a robust software throwing alerts is essential for effective identification and reporting of suspicious transactions.

NBFCs were advised to initiate urgent steps to ensure electronic filing of cash transaction report (CTR) and Suspicious Transaction Reports (STR) to FIU-IND.

NBFCs are to make Cash Transaction Reports (CTR) to FIU-India for every month latest by 15th of the succeeding month. For determining integrally connected cash transactions, NBFCs should take into account all individual cash transactions *in an account during a calendar month*, where either debit or credit summation, computed separately, exceeds rupees ten lakh during the month.

NBFCs are required to pay special attention to all complex, unusual large transactions and all unusual patterns of transactions, which have no apparent economic or visible lawful purpose. It is further clarified that the background including all documents/office records/memorandums pertaining to such transactions and purpose thereof should, as far as possible, be examined and the findings at branch as well as Principal Officer level should be properly recorded. These records are required to be preserved for ten years as is required under PMLA, 2002. Such records and related documents should be made available to help auditors in their work relating to scrutiny of transactions and also to Reserve Bank/other relevant authorities.

In paragraph 7 of our April 5, 2006 circular, NBFCs have been advised that the customer should not be tipped off on the STRs made by them to FIU-IND. It is likely that in some cases transactions are abandoned/aborted by customers on being asked to give some details or to provide documents. It is clarified that NBFCs should report all such *attempted transactions in STRs*, even if not completed by customers, irrespective of the amount of the transaction.

While making STRs, NBFCs should be guided by the definition of 'suspicious transaction' as contained in Rule 2(g) of Rules *ibid.* It is further clarified that NBFCs should make STRs if they have reasonable ground to believe that the transaction involve proceeds of crime generally *irrespective of the amount of transaction* and/or the threshold limit envisaged for predicate offences in part B of Schedule of PMLA, 2002.

These guidelines are issued under Sections 45K and 45L of the Reserve Bank of India Act, 1934. Any contravention of the said guidelines may attract penalties under the relevant provisions of the Act:

(i) As per above clarification, the debit transactions in the above example are integrally connected cash transactions because total cash debits during the calendar month exceeds Rs. 10 lakh. However, the NBFC should report only the debit transaction taken place on 02/04 and 08/04/2008. The debit transaction dated 07/04/2008 should not be separately reported by the NBFC, which is less than Rs. 50,000.

(ii) All the credit transactions in the above example would not be treated as integrally connected, as the sum total of the credit transactions during the month does not exceed Rs. 10 lakh and hence credit transaction dated 02, 07 and 08/04/2008 should not be reported by NBFC.

An Indicative List of Suspicious Activities and Transactions Involving Large Amounts of Cash

Company transactions, that are denominated by unusually large amounts of cash, rather than normally associated with the normal commercial operations of the company, e.g. cheques.

Transactions that do not make Economic Sense

Transactions in which assets are withdrawn immediately after being deposited unless the business activities of the customers furnishes a plausible reason for immediate withdrawal.

Activities not Consistent with the Customer's Business

Accounts with large volume of credits whereas the nature of business does not justify such credits.

Attempts to Avoid Reporting/Record-keeping Requirements

(i) A customer who is reluctant to provide information needed for a mandatory report, to have the report filed or to proceed with a transaction after being informed that the report must be filed.
(ii) Any individual or group that coerces/induces or attempts to coerce/induce a NBFC employee not to file any reports or any other forms.
(iii) An account where there are several cash transactions below a specified threshold level to avoid filing of reports that may be necessary in case of transactions above the threshold level, as the customer intentionally splits the transaction into smaller amounts for the purpose of avoiding the threshold limit.

Unusual Activities

Funds coming from the countries/centres which are known for money laundering.

Customer who Provides Insufficient or Suspicious Information

(i) A customer/company who is reluctant to provide complete information regarding the purpose of the business, prior business relationships, officers or directors, or its locations.
(ii) A customer/company who is reluctant to reveal details about its activities or to provide financial statements.
(iii) A customer who has no record of past or present employment but makes frequent large transactions.

Certain NBFC Employees Arousing Suspicion

(i) An employee whose lavish lifestyle cannot be supported by his or her salary.
(ii) Negligence of employees/wilful blindness is reported repeatedly.

CONSUMER PROTECTION ACT

Multi-Level Marketing Companies merchandise schemes are ultimately targeting the consumers of fast moving consumer goods. Any consumer products can be sold at the soaring price set by the fraudsters if it is supported by the tools of heavy commission offers and downline enrollment. The end consumers are destined to purchase the unwanted products at exorbitant price. The Consumer Protection Act of India also incorporates some provisions to take on the MLM.

The Act promulgated in the year 1986 with the objective of protecting the consumers from immoral practice of business organizations. Companies who becomes monopolies in the market make gains by resorting to cheating and market frauds, utilizing the monopoly powers.

Against such situation, Consumer Protection Act provides that the consumers should have right to get information of quality, quantity and price of products. Consumer can sue in district forum and complaint against the cheating of businessmen. The Act is aimed at educating the consumers regarding their rights and powers.

Section 1.2 of the Act defines a consumer to be any person who buys any goods for a consideration which has been paid or promised. Besides the actual purchaser consumer includes the user of such products. It also includes person who hires or avails of any services and other beneficiaries who made payment wholly or partly.

The end consumers in the MLM schemes will come within the meaning of the term 'consumer' and are thus entitled to get all the rights of the consumers. He can sue the companies for the sale of cheating products. But once he starts selling the same products creating his own downline, his status gradually changes.

The trade practice followed by the MLM companies are deceptive and unfair. The following practices resorted to by the MLM companies for promoting sales will come within the purview of Deceptive and Unfair Trade Practices defined under section[1]. 4-1 of the Consumer Protection Act.

1. The practice of making statement in the business meets and advertisement with the help of audio and video representation which:
   (a) Falsely represent the quality and grade of the products.
   (b) Falsely represent that the quality of the services provided by the companies.
   (c) Falsely represents the old piling stock of the companies to be new good.
   (d) Falsely represents that the standard of the product is certified (like ISO certification).
   (e) Falsely represent that the sellers has a sponsorship or approval or affiliation. (The companies normally claim that they are affiliated to World Trade Centre, Member of FICCI, affiliated to some Government organizations, members of Direct Selling Associations, Guineas World Record in networking and so on.)
   (f) Makes false or misleading statement concerning the need for or the usefulness of any goods or services provided by them.
   (g) Gives to the public any warranty or guarantee for the durability and standard of the product that is not based on an adequate or proper test thereof.
   (h) Makes to the public a promise of buyback or replacement or maintenance if such warranty meant to mislead the consumers without any reasonable prospect that such promise will be carried out. Buyback offers of the MLM companies are not practically carried out.
   (i) Any misleading statement regarding the price of the products sold by it or like products available in the market.
   (j) Gives false or misleading facts disparaging the goods, services or trade of another person.
2. Makes advertisement in the print or visual media regariding the price at which the goods and services are offered and at the same time compelling the public to become member of

the scheme and consequently to purchase the product at the high rates at which sales are made to members. Section 2 of the Consumer Protection Act can be interpreted to attract this practice of the MLM companies.

3. Permits offering of gifts or prize with the intention of not providing them actually or creating impression that something is being given free when it is actually covered by the price. The selling scheme of MLM companies incorporates these sorts of offering of prizes.
4. Permits the sale or supply of goods intended to be used by consumers knowing that the goods do not comply with the standards prescribed by competent authorities relating to performance composition contents design packing etc.

Section 2(1)(n) of the Consumer Protection Act defines a Restrictive Trade Practice to be any trade practice which requires a consumer to buy or hire of any goods or services as a condition precedent for buying or hiring of other goods or services. Thus, where sale or purchase of a product or service is made conditional on the sale or purchase of other products and services it amounts to restrictive trade practice.

Such kinds of tie-up sales or tying arrangements are typical of the companies running product based MLM. The ultimate effect is that a purchase is forced to buy some goods or services which he does not require along with the goods which he wants to buy. The buyer forego his free choice between competing products and this neutralized healthy competition in the tied market.

SALE OF GOODS ACT

The companies running pyramid schemes based on cheating products can be held responsible in the civil court using the provisions of Indian Sale of Goods Act, 1930. Every sale is a contract between seller and buyer. Section 4(1) of the Act defines "this contract of sale of goods as a contract whereby the seller transfers or agrees to transfer the property in goods to the buyer for a price."

The terms such as goods, buyer, seller, price, property and sale are defined in this Act and along with the Consumer Protection Act it gives the members who lose in the scheme a tool for suing the companies.

Freezing of Assets

Fund accumulated by the companies in their bank accounts, by illegal means have to be confiscated as benefit of crime, under the provision of Cr.PC. It wound be legal on the part of the investigating officers to freeze the bank account of the company directors under section 102 Cr.P.C.

Section 105C defines "proceeds of crime" to be any property derived or obtained directly or indirectly by any person as a result of criminal activity or the value of any such property. "Property" includes assets of every description whether corporeal or incorporeal, movable or immovable, tangible or intangible, derived or used in the Commission of an Offence and includes property obtained through proceeds of crime.

Any proceeds of Crime or Property obtained using proceeds of crime can be attached or forfeited under the provisions of *sections 105D* to *105J.* Such attachment order of the Court can be executed through the Court or revenue authority in the State where the property is situated.

But some of Court orders interpreting these provision to be applicable only to those properties situated in foreign countries leaves the investigating officers helpless in attaching the properties. This is an area where loopholes in the existing law needs rectification. However, with regard to the illegally acquired properties in foreign countries the attachment provision can be invoked.

Any letter of request in this regard received by the Central Government from a Court or an authority in a contracting State may be forwarded to the Court, as it thinks fit, for execution in accordance with the provisions of sections 105D to 105J. Section 105D confers powers to the Court to direct the Police Officers not below the rank of Sub Inspectors to trace the property obtained using proceeds of crime.

Property Attachment by Investigating Officers

Section 105E of Cr.P.C. confers power to the police officers conducting an inquiry or investigation for making an order of attachment directing that such property shall not be transferred or otherwise dealt with, except with the prior permission of the officer. This can be invoked if the investigating officer has reason to believe that any property is likely to be concealed, transferred or dealt with in any manner which will result in the disposal of such property before completing such investigation. Investigating officer shall serve a copy of such order to the concerned person.

Any such order has to be confirmed by an order of the Court within a period of thirty days.

The District Magistrate or any other officer nominated by him, of the area where property is situated can be appointed by the Court for the proper management and administration of the seized or forfeited property. The administrator shall receive and manage the property as may be specified by the Central Government. He can take measures, as directed by Central Government, to dispose of the forfeited property.

Notice of Forfeiture of Property

If the Court is convinced that whole or part of such property is proceeds of crime on the basis of inquiry or investigation findings, it may serve a notice upon such person seeking explanation for the source of income, earning or assets, and can ask for show cause as to why such properties, should not be declared to be proceeds of crime and forfeited to the Central Government. Copy of notice shall also be served on such person who is holding possession of such property.

After considering the explanation to such notice and the material evidences before it, and after hearing the affected person, the Court may by order record a finding whether all or any of the properties are proceeds of crime. Such proceedings can be done *ex parte* if the concerned person does not appear before the Court within thirty days of receiving the show cause notice on the basis of evidence available before it. Where the Court records a finding that any property is proceeds of crime, such property shall stand forfeited to the Central Government free from all encumbrances. Where any share in a company stand forfeited to the Central Government, the company, forthwith registers the Central Government as the transferee of such shares.

The Court can make an order giving an option to the person affected to pay, in lieu of forfeiture, a fine equal to the market value of such property, in a case where only part of the property is found to be proceeds of crime. This can be done after giving reasonable opportunity to the concerned person for being heard. The Court can revoke the declaration of forfeiture of such property if such fine is paid within the specified time. If any property in respect of which forfeiture order has come or notice is served is transferred by any mode, such transfer shall be deemed to be null and void.

Indian Judicial Review

Over the three decades of its existence, through series of judgments, Indian Courts have developed some effective norms for interpreting the Prize Chits and Money Circulation Scheme Banning Act and have approached the suits relating to MLM companies with more caution. Considering the huge economic stakes held by the MLM companies and the extent of mass affected by the schemes even this cautionary approach in interpreting the existing laws has become inadequate. New legislation is warranted for a total ban of the MLM business. The following are the landmark judgments made by the Indian Courts:

1. Swapan Kumar Guha V/s *State of Bengal*

The Hon. Supreme Court of India, in the case of Swapan Kumar Guha *V/s* State of Bengal, had made the following observation if the offence under these sections is to attract.

There must be a scheme.

There must be members in the scheme.

The scheme must be for the making of quick and easy money contingent on an event or contingency relative to the enrollment of new members into the scheme or there must be a scheme for the receipt of money as consideration for a promise to pay money relative to the enrollment of members into the scheme.

This judgement clarifies the legal requirement for bringing conviction to a person who runs or promotes or enrolls a pyramid scheme. It must be proved that a person is promoting or conducting a scheme for making of quick or easy money and the chance of making easy money must be depending on the enrollment of members into the scheme. This judgment was promulgated in the year 1982 and the so-called Multi-Level Marketing has not become so prominent during that period.

2. Amway India V/s *Union of India, High Court of AP 2007 (4)*

MLM has recently come under the judicial scrutiny in some High Courts across the country. The dispute involving Amway was heard by the Andhra Pradesh High Court in 2007.

The primary legal framework governing such situations is the Prize Chits and Money Circulation Schemes (Banning) Act, 1978, under which 'Money Circulation Scheme' is defined [Section 2(c)]. The Court, in examining the ingredients of the Section laid down a two-step test—firstly, it must be proved that first petitioner is promoting or conducting a scheme for the making of quick or easy money, and second, the chance or opportunity of making quick or easy money must be shown to depend upon an event or contingency relative or applicable to enrollment of members into that scheme.

The scheme of the business operation of Amway, very simply, is that the money that the sponsor member at the top of the line gets depend upon members whom he enrolls or the members enrolled by him enroll. Therefore, although enrollment of new members is not the purported criteria for the scheme, the scheme is structured in a manner such that inherently, there is sufficient inducement for aggressive enrollment of new members.

The return of any sponsor is calculated not only on the basis of his own sales, but also on the performance of the members recruited by him. Furthermore, to be eligible for the commission, minimum business levels have to be maintained, which require aggressively recruiting new members.

The requirements of 'Money Circulation Scheme' such as offering of easy money and an element of contingency for such returns upon the enrollment of new downline members etc. are met in respect of the Amway sales scheme. The scheme is almost identical with the pyramid scheme. The Hon. Andhra Pradesh High Court held that the Amway scheme is illegal and the Apex Court of the land have upheld this ruling.

3. Kuriachan Chacko V/s *State of Kerala*

Hon. Justice Basant of Kerala High Court while interpreting the LIS case, Kuriachan Chacko *vs.* State of Kerala, had unleashed scathing criticism against the previous interpretations of the Act and had observed that Multi-Level Marketing is nothing but camouflaged money circulation scheme.

This landmark judgement was upheld by the Hon. Supreme Court of India, in the year 2008 [Reported in 2008 (8) SC Journal page 708].

Similar observations came from Indian Courts in Gemini Techno Marketing *vs.* Union of India. WP 22914 of AP High Court and Apple FMCG *vs.* State of T.N. & Ors, 2005 (Madras High Court).

Sri Balwinder Singh, a retired IPS Officer and adviser to the Ministry of Corporate Affairs have proposed some norms for identifying illegal schemes and they are the following:

If a scheme envisages certain deposit/entry fee or periodical subscription etc. and the scheme provides commission/incentive for enrolling members then the scheme is a violation of the Money Circulation (Banning) Act.

If a scheme provides for earning of commission on sale of products/services only on the condition that the participant would have to enroll certain minimum number of members then also the scheme is violation of the Money Circulation (Banning) Act.

If the scheme is so conceived that it induces enrollment of new members to earn more and more commission, i.e. if the 'upline' members in the pyramid get commission on the business turned out by the 'downline' members then also it is violation of the Money Circulation (Banning) Act.

New Legislation in the States

Some, of the State Governments have proposed a bill at the instigation of Indian Direct Selling Association in the guise of 'controlling' the MLM. This in continuation of the guidelines issued by the State Governments when MLM business have come to the limelight in the wake of a series of cases registered nation-wide against the various companies in early 2011 and 2012 at the auspices of the state police in States like, Kerala, Andhra Pradesh, Maharashtra, Delhi etc.

Even when the Draft Bill is aimed at controlling the Direct Selling Entities, it is very strange to see that the Concept of Direct Selling is not defined anywhere in the Act. Also illegal entity Multi-Level Marketing is not defined in the Act. Any legislation dealing with MLM and Direct Selling will become ineffective if the law does not say what it is.

To be legitimate direct sellers and not just pyramid sellers, the majority of product sales must be to non-participants who are not authorized to make further recruitments. No illegal practice of endless chain recruitment can be controlled without incorporating such a provision. In the absence of such a provision the heavy burden of commission payment will lie on the end consumers in the camouflaged form of high price.

This would be a good place to post the requirement that MLM direct sellers be able to furnish proof through sale receipts that over 50 per cent (or 70% would be even better) of sales are to non-participants who are not authorized to sell products or recruit others.

Though the draft bill does not include such provision, there are some protections against "pay-to-play" requirements, which cause participants much loss (Provision IV and V in the Kerala Draft Bill).

But the provision in the draft that *"It shall not restrict the number of distributors that can be registered or enrolled as direct sellers"* will permit the MLM companies to recruit as many distributors as possible. Actually, such restriction could help to prevent market saturation. The above provision would make the state to be the first in the world to make the endless chain system legitimate.

MLM companies should be required to furnish average NET payout to ALL participants at all levels in the pay plan. In other words, money received from the company in commissions and bonuses minus money paid to participants by the company for products, training, lead generation systems etc. Taylor says this figure is nearly always negative. And it would be important that ALL who signed up are included in the average figures, not just those who are currently active.

A list of references of participants in their area would be helpful, including some who dropped out. Also, a waiting period of 7 days would be helpful to give prospects a chance to go to the Internet and check out the company.

The consumers would be better off if MLM were banned altogether.

References

1. RBI/2004-05/302 UBD.PCB. Cir.30/09.161.00/2004-05.
2. RBI Circular no 2004-05/284-DBOD. NO. AML.BC.58/14.01.001/2004-05.
3. RBI/2009-10/158 UBD. CO.BPD. PCB. Cir. No.9/12.05.001/2009-10 dated September 16, 2009.

15
Setting Out a Legal Framework for the Anti-Money Siphoning Enforcement

The early detection and successful prosecution of the illegal investment scheme, requires some paraphernalia like availability of professional investigators, prosecutors, judicial officers as well as other resources. There are some institutional preconditions for enforcement of anti-money siphoning laws. The dearth of this in several legal regimes prevents proactive legal response from the regulators. The money chain companies thrive in an atmosphere where there is no effective mechanism to detect and monitor illegal investment schemes. The drive against such companies will be handicapped if there are no clear-cut laws that ensure punishment for the guilty.

What comes in the way of strong regulations for checking the fraud practices is the lack of political and popular support for such laws. The legal system will swing into action to frame strong laws against uncontrolled investment schemes and multi-level marketing only if a volcanic eruption of anger of victims takes to the street. But public at large is still not woken up to dangers of mammoth-sized frauds that put in peril not just individuals but the economy as a whole in some cases.

The con companies have found out innovative ways to cover up their nefarious designs. They actively intervene in philanthropic activities by donating fund for various charity activities. They splurge money on such activities mainly as a public relations exercise. When confronted with the law enforcing agencies, these companies would highlight their humanitarian concerns, cleverly hiding their blood-sucking face. The public perception of these companies is also, by and large, moulded by their publicity blitzkrieg.

Ample Powers to the Investigators

As the situation is loaded against them, the investigators should be given the mandate to act against such companies independently without additional approval from the government. This becomes all the more important if the fraudulent schemes are launched with the tacit support of those who have some connection with the government.

Taking on the firms that are spread across the countries is not an easy task. They will exploit all the legal avenues to wriggle out of the judicial process. This will invariably land the investigators into the cobweb of litigations and protracted legal fights in their personal capacities. So, it is imperative that there should be enough provisions in the law to salvage the investigators from the litigations that could arise while discharging their duties.

Stopping the fraudulent schemes is impossible if the enforcement is not supported by political and popular will. Financial regulators lack popular support due to several reasons. Complexity of the scheme leads to limited understanding of its ramifications. The damage caused by these frauds to the economy is not properly subjected to media attention. The sponsoring of programme for governmental or social causes like sports, beauty contests, charities and even political campaigns by the companies earns them public support.

Against this backdrop only financial regulators with unfettered powers and sufficient independence can cope with the mandates of high profile investigation.

Un-Ambiguous Law with Comprehensive Provisions

The statues of the nations should have clear provisions for prosecuting the schemers and the punishment should be deterrent. All the probable course of actions followed by the fraudsters are to be specifically defined to be cognizable offence in the law. Collection of deposit from the public without authority, offering of excessive return, public offering of securities and setting of prices not according to the market forces of demand and supply are all to be made the prime concern of such legislation. Licensing and Registration system can be introduced for a wide spectrum of activities.

There has to be clear provisions in the law to ban sale of worthless products using the tool of chair referral, Sale of products at incomparable prices of similar products, schemes compelling mandatory purchase or periodical subscription, incentive system leading to inventory loading etc.

Ability to Track Fund

The most important aspect of investigation in the Collective Investment Scheme is Tracking of Fund and the ability of the investigator depends on the authority to access information and data from various institutions like Banks, Insurance Companies, Stock Broking Firms and Foreign Exchange Firms etc. Successful prosecutions of fraud cases depend on the recovery of money from the financial institutions where perpetrators might have shifted the booty taken from the public. There is a variety of mechanism for transferring the funds to cross boarder accounts like *hawala* exchange. There has to be provisions for bringing back the money or to freeze the accounts in foreign banks. Attaching properties situated in foreign countries is practically impossible now-a-days. All these complex issues call for a greater level of international co-operation.

Availability of Civil Solutions

Enforcement will be crippled in the absence of instant Civil Remedies, along with criminal prosecution which is a time consuming process. The fraudsters are using unheard of practices to hoodwink the investigators and relying solely on the criminal prosecution, which depends on evidences, is not the panacea for combating economic crimes. If the perpetrators can safeguard the booty despite facing criminal charges, the enforcement becomes meaningless. Vesting of both civil and administrative powers on the enforcement agencies help in speedy attaching of properties, appointing of receivers for taking care of such properties etc. There has to be provision for disposing of the property and disbursing the proceeds to the investors. Sending the culprits behind bars would be an additional deterrence.

Empowering the enforcement to initiate civil and criminal proceedings simultaneously is inevitable to crack down on the entities.

This alone will avoid the recurrence such scams. Penalties should be some multiples of the amounts collected by the culprits.

Inter-National Co-operation

Several of the schemes are being run by transnational corporations with their branches in several continents. Net working and pyramiding is extended from one country to another and against this backdrop the countries are to co-operate and co-ordinate on their action against Ponzi Scheme.[1] Enforcement will be crippled in the absence of an Inter-National Agency vested with powers of busting the fraudsters and confiscating the assets and repatriate it to the homeland proportionate to the percentage of collection made from different jurisdictions.

A co-ordinate strategy is required for exchanging of information relating to bank accounts and funds, confidential verification of the asset backing of the companies, exchanging of accused etc. which will lead to more effective enforcement.

United Nations Convention against Transnational Organized Crime, Palermo Convention, aims to promote international co-operation in preventing and combating these sorts of crimes more effectively. The Convention will help the member countries to get international co-operation in tracing, seizure, freezing, and confiscation of the proceeds of crimes. A wide range of mutual legal assistance treaties are being signed under this. This movement requires further momentum for combating covert and overt pyramid and Ponzi schemes.

Emergency Relief

Prompt attachment of property by the investigative agency even without the presence or written complaint of the plaintiff, is the only solution for preventing its alienation. The need for seeking prior court's approval will only delay the procedure. There is need for greater co-operation between the financial regulators and the criminal enforcement authorities. Criminal law enforcement should have authority to close down the schemes.

It is a time consuming process to complete a full investigation to bring civil/administrative or criminal charges against unregulated schemes. By that time it is likely that scheme operators will vanish with the investors' money or else it will be relocated to other jurisdictions with the possibility of making repatriation difficult. Thus, once a fraudulent investment scheme is detected regulatory authority should go for the emergency relief of temporary injunctions and the freezing of assets. Even when the investigation aimed at bringing charges continues, these emergency steps will protect the depositor's interest. There has to be mechanism for restitution of money or property recovered, if any, to the investors.

Professionally Competent Investigators

In many a jurisdiction, tackling of ponzi schemes have not yet started. It requires lot of experience for police personnel to initiate prosecution. Crime of pyramid schemes reached new dimensions applying modern technology, complicated designs, and expertise in multi-disciplinary subjects. It is a real challenge as only a very few are competent to handle the crimes requiring deep technological analysis, account works and adducing of soft evidences. Application of cyber forensic tools of investigation, digital surveillance and tracking of accused, seizing the database of the fraudulent domains and presenting them as offline website before the court and adducing of other soft evidences are all the inevitable process of investigation in these crimes. Without creating a quality manpower, enforcement will become a mockery in front of high tech criminals.

Internal manuals of investigation are to be drafted. Also investigators should have professional competence to allow them to leverage their resources in order to detect investment fraud conducted *via* the internet.

Specialized Judicial Officers

The uncontrolled investment schemes can brought to successful prosecution only if there are sufficient number of special courts for dealing with economic offences. Judges should have the necessary expertise for speedy disposition of financial matters. It requires special attention by governments as the administrative set-up of lower judiciary is derailed with heavy burden of under trial cases. Under-staffed and over-stretched judicial systems cannot cope with the challenges. Specialization by judicial officers is inevitable.

Proactive Investigation

Many an investment schemes are run with the investors themselves aware of its illegality. Exorbitant return received by the senior members prompt them to keep the operation secret and the newly enrolled members also will be instructed to keep the confidentiality. Under such situation the information furnished by the investors will be scanty and is thus not easy to detect.

Investigators responsibility is to create confidence in the minds of the losers to give complaint. Senior leaders will unleash propaganda that the funds will be returned only to those who does not approach the enforcement agencies.

In many a jurisdiction enrolling into such schemes itself amounts to criminal offence. This make it impossible for the members to state before the investigators that they have enrolled into the scheme. There has to be provision for treating the members in the lower strata who did not go for further enrollment as witness as otherwise successful prosecution will be impossible.

Fraud Watch

There has to be continuous system of fraud watch. It should have the capacity to detect the frauds basing on some symptoms. The existence of a Ponzi or Pyramid Scheme can be identified with the help of these symptoms which include promises of high return guarantees, low risk, availability only to members, lack of registration, lack of financial information, affinity frauds aimed at religious or ethnic groups; lack of clear and detailed explanations; lack of background information on promoters; and pressure to reinvest etc.

Technical Surveillance

There has to be some agency entrusted with the task of developing some technical tools for facilitating search on the internet as well as other mass media for detecting the fraudulent schemes. Fraudsters appeal to investors *via* advertisements in newspapers or television. Thus, it is important that regulatory agencies develop mechanisms and tools that allow them to monitor such advertisements and websites.

Public Awareness

There has to be awareness campaigns on pyramid and other similar schemes for sensitizing members of the public. The general public and the investment community need to have a better understanding of the working mechanism of capital market and the financial regulations in the country. The rules to be complied by the investors and those relating to financial market tools are to be propagated among the public. Enforcement agencies should promote confidence in the public and members of the scheme to provide oral, written and electronic complaints to the authorities.

The enforcement agencies should have expertise to give opinion about a particular scheme as to how it defraud investors. Viability of the schemes can be judged on the basis of several objective norms which are to be published in the official website of the police department. List of institutions or entities *that* hold or do not hold a licence to carry out financial activities can be published. The action taken against the schemes and the illogic methods employed by the fraudsters can be published in the office sites.

The nature of the pyramid schemes, its un-viability and the identity of the directors and the names of such un-viable schemes operating in the country etc. can be listed.

Prevention of Benami Transactions

The funds raised through illegal schemes are often laundered through proxy accounts. There are instances where the huge funds accumulated through the fraud schemes are deposited in the accounts of layman who is not at all aware of such accounts. It is seen that land extending nearly 135 acres are found in the name of a proxy director of the company Tycoon Empire International. Such were not isolated examples.

Thus, there has to be specific laws in all the countries for preventing such *benami* accounts and to freeze the assets in such accounts. In India, the Benami Transaction (Prohibition) Act undertakes this issue. It defines *benami* property and a *benami* transaction to be a transaction or agreement where a property is transferred to or held by a person for a consideration provided or paid by another person. Such a property is held for the immediate or future benefit, direct or indirect, of the person providing the consideration. A transaction or arrangement in respect of a property carried out or made in a fictitious name or where the owner of the property is not aware of or denies knowledge of such ownership is also included in the definition of *benami* transaction. The Act provides for confiscation of the *benami* property and a punishment to the concerned for an imprisonment up to two years in addition to a fine.

The procedure for enquiry and determination of *benami* property and its consequences need to be specifically defined.

Enhancing the Accountability of Auditors

Many of the offences would not have been possible had the auditors were accountable. Cases are detected regularly by the regulatory authorities, involving highly reputed corporate, where the Auditors have failed to point out gross violations and even blatant misrepresentations. In the absence of adequate effective provisions, the Auditors are hardly ever held accountable for these lapses. A strict Auditor ready to blow the whistle can hardly expect to thrive amidst competitors and thus many of them are more than willing to co-operate and compromise at different levels. As a result, a very important regulatory tool is virtually losing its role in contributing towards greater compliance.

The functioning of professionals including auditors, company secretaries and bankers need be continuously monitored and any apathetic approach on their side is to be legally dealt with. Ensuring the accountability of these professionals is a prerequisite for any enforcement against the unregulated investment schemes. Attesting the declarations, statements without understanding the ramifications or deliberately connivance to the companies for running fraudulent schemes should definitely bring the auditors also into conviction.

Reference

1. Ponzi Schemes in the Carribean: Ana Carvajal, Hunter Monroe, Catherine Pattilo and Brian Wynter—*IMF Working Paper*.

16
Crime Investigation

In the absence of system of continuous quake watch with clear and easy intelligible norms for identifying the various forms of complicated schemes, regulatory frameworks will be crippled. Collection of evidence and bringing the accused to successful prosecution requires a clear understanding of the scheme. Though the evidence in a particular case depends on the nature of scheme offered by the company against whom case is registered, some general guidelines and methodology can be set forth for the investigation of these new *modus operandi* economic offences

The First Information Report

It has been asserted by various courts that early detection and stopping the investment plans of various forms of money circulation scheme is the *bona fide* duty of the police and thus, it is fair on the part of the police to register FIR *suo motu* without waiting for the complaints from the victim.

A specific description of the nature of the scheme offered by the accused company or persons is to be provided in the First Information statement. The category of the plan based on enrollment pattern, as to whether it is following Binary, matrix, revolving matrix, auto filling or generation plan etc. are to be narrated in the FIR itself. The unviability and infeasibility of the offered scheme may be explained as far as possible.

The content of easy money offer and enrollment of new members by the existing members is to be described in the FIR. The unlimited enrollment nature and exorbitant price of the products sold need be explained in the FIR.

The Section of Laws Invoked

An element of cheating is there in all the unregulated investment schemes. The intention of cheating the investors is evident from the very designing of the plan. Wrongful loss to the downline members and wrongful gain to the fraudulent directors is a prominent feature of these schemes and thus invoking section 420 IPC is warranted in all the cases. There is ruling by Calcutta High Court that in the absence of cheating intention even money circulation scheme is legal. The fraudsters resort to forging of soft and hard documents for the running of the scheme these forged documents will be used as though genuine. Depending on the presence of this aspect sections 468 and 471 IPC can be invoked.

Enrolling in a money circulation scheme and promoting it is an offence under sections 3 and 5 of Prize, Chits and Money Circulation Scheme (Banning) Act, 1978. Offence done by the companies is punishable under section 6 of the PCMC Act and thus companies are to be arrayed as accused in the cases.

Almost all the schemes are run with the help of a website and the scheme is presented in website. Cheating by personating using computer and internet is to be dealt with by invoking 66D of IT Act. Any SMS or write up promoting or propagating the money circulation scheme will attract section 5 (c) (3) of PCMC Act.

Violations of SEBI Act, section 11A relating to collective investment, provisions in the Companies Act relating to the issuing of share, violation of memorandum and articles of association, provisions of RBI Act, Sections 45J, 45NA, 45S etc. relating to restrictions on the receipt of deposits etc. are discussed in the chapter MLM against the Backdrop of Indian Law.

Accused

The directors or shareholders enlisted in the memorandum and articles of association are to be arrayed as accused in the case. Besides this all the senior leaders in the scheme who have promoted the scheme by enrolling downline members are to be arrayed as accused. As the offence done by the companies is specifically defined in the Act, companies are to be arrayed as accused. In many a cases, the directors will be the obedient coolie workers under the real culprits and in such cases confining the list of accused to proxy directors is not enough.

Evidence from the Registrar of Companies

Most of the companies are registered with the Registrar of Companies under the Ministry of Corporate Affairs of the Government of India. Investigation against the fraudulent scheme run by the companies can be started from the Registrar of Companies. Notice under section 91 Cr.P.C can be issued to ROC for furnishing the certified copies or soft copies of the following documents:

1. Certificate of Incorporation document issued by the ROC to a Company and this will contain the incorporation number.
2. Articles of Association.
3. Memorandum of Association.
4. Form 32 for appointment, promotion and cessation of directors.
5. Form 18 showing the address of the registered office of the companies.
6. Annual Return statements etc.

Articles and Memorandum of Association will give the list of directors who registered the companies. Form 32 is to be filed in respect of each director at the time of appointment, promotion and cessation. These are the primary documents to prove the gang behind the scheme. Form 18 will specify the registered address of the firm and whenever the office is shifted Form 18 is to be filed. The rising of fund by the companies can be proved with the annual return statement.

Several other associate companies will be registered by the master company doing the money circulation scheme for facilitating siphoning of fund and thus, corresponding documents of all the associate firms are to be seized from the Registrar of Companies.

Evidence from the Bankers

The subscribers/promoters/agents in various schemes are generally remitting the payments to the bank account of the company. Wherever complaints are coming, information has to be taken as to which account the payments are made by the members. The bank will be at the headquarters town where the company is situated. Notice under section 91 Cr.P.C. is to be issued to the Bank Manager for providing the following details:

1. Account Transaction Statement, containing the details of total cumulative deposits, total cumulative withdrawal and balance as on date of each account.
2. Account opening forms submitted to the bank by the account holder, who will normally be the director of the company. A specimen signature form with photo of the account holder and resolution of the company authorizing the particular director to operate the account will also be attached to the account opening forms.
3. Customer Master Forms in respect of each director authorized to operate the account.

These documents constitute the primary evidence against the company and the volume of fraud. In most of the cases the company directors will be the account holders.

Commission, Bonus, Loyalty etc. offered by the company will be disbursed to the investors through RTGS from the same account. Thus, Account Transaction Statement of the senior leaders of the scheme also has to be taken for understanding as to how much amount he has received from the company. Return flow of money from company's account to the accounts of various investors can be proved by the company's account transaction statements. This will help in understanding the culpability, in terms of return, of a promoter. Separate observation Mahazar can be prepared in respect of each accused.

Proving the Website

There will be a website which can be accessed to by entering the secret user ID and Password assigned to each investor. Archiving this site with the help of high tech cell is to be done without any loss of time because immediately with the news of registering crime access to this site will be blocked by the company. If the site is deleted from the net 204 IPC can be incorporated as it will amount to tampering of evidence.

Evidence from the Web Hosting Companies

Proving the Website Ownership

The ownership of the domain with the help of which the scheme was run is to be proved. Investigation has to be extended to the web hosting companies. They can give evidence regarding the ownership of the website. The agreement showing the terms and conditions with the domain reselling firm is to be seized.

Seizing Data Base

The data base of the company website has to be seized in the case. Back up of data base will be available with the system administrator of the company, web hosting company or the server company. The memory device should be properly sealed in the presence of the witness. The seized memory devise is to be produced before the court.

Cyber Forensic Examination

The seized memory devise is to be sent to the FSL for cyber forensic analysis. The expert may be requested to take a mirror image of the memory, to convert the same into an offline website and to issue certificate regarding the basic features of the website. A sample of the entry in the forwarding note regarding the nature of examination required is provided along with this.

Presenting Database as Offline Website

The original data base returned from the FSL can be converted into a website in a laptop with a Server Operating System, during trial so that the court can take judicial notice of the various aspects of the website. Either Cyber Forensic Expert or any other local expert who can do this work from the court hall is to be cited as witness in the case. If it is done during investigation stage, if trial is delayed, it may not function properly by that time.

Seizing Investigation Copy of Data Base

It is inevitable to have the website for the investigation work. As accessing of the memory devise after seizure will adversely affect the evidentiary value, separate copy may be seized for the investigation work. If investigation copy is not seized from any source, cyber expert may be requested to issue a copy of the same. The Investigation Officer can convert the investigation copy into a website and can use the same for investigation work.

Submitting Printout of Relevant Pages vide Observation Mahazar

Printout has to be taken of all the soft pages where evidence against the accused is found. For example the details of the business plan offered by the company can be taken from the site. Also by accessing the site with the user ID and Password of a member from the user log in side, pages will appear like the profile of a member, income earned by a member, no. of persons sponsored by a member etc. Wherever printouts are seized the link of the soft page in the website has to be shown in the *mahazar*.

Evidence From Internet

The website, *www.web.archive.org* owned by the American government archives all the open pages of the websites available in the net. Print outs of Home page, business plan page etc. can be taken from the website *vide an* observation *mahazar* and the Court may be requested to take judicial notice of these links.

If the website is available, whenever a person is arrested evidence in respect of that accused, including the number of persons enrolled in the scheme by him presented in the form of a binary tree, payout history, E-wallet, matching bonus, loyalty bonus paid to him etc., will be available from the web page which can be accessed by entering the secret User ID and Password assigned to the investor. The soft page should be downloaded into a memory device and the same has to be prepared in the model of a Recovery *Mahazar* under section 27 Evidence Act. Also hard copy has to be submitted to the Court. The details of the link of web page have to be explained in the body of *mahazar*. The part of confession revealing the secret user ID and Password are admissible evidence and the same has to be produced before the Court.

In respect of the companies which are actually selling products, the pyramid structure of organization form, easy money offer, enrolling of new members by the person who purchases a product etc. has to be brought out in the witness statement. Normally, the price of such products will be abnormally high and barring the actual price of the product, the balance amount will work as the investment in the money circulation scheme. Thus, price of the product has to be specifically mentioned in the statements of witnesses.

Some companies had designed some cheating products for camouflaging their money circulation scheme. The products like nano bracelet, jewel watch, alcohol card, tobacco card etc. are really of no value and are sold at a very high price. Here also the sale of product is meant only for covering up the money circulation scheme. Expert opinion can be taken on the ingredients of the product to prove that it does not have any value.

It is observed that in various cases only those whose names are mentioned in the FIR are arrayed as accused. An investor can prefer petition against the promoter who enrolled him in the scheme. In the investigation the tentacles upward are to be tracked and arrayed as accused. In all the different schemes the real beneficiaries are the senior leaders in the chain. The senior leaders in the scheme in all the districts are to be arrayed as the accused in the cases registered in that district.

The accused shall not be allowed to enjoy the benefit of crime and thus provisions under section 102 Cr.P.C. is to be invoked for attaching the bank deposits of the company earned through this illegal scheme. Letter has to be given to all the Bank Managers for freezing the account of the company. The Registrar and village officers are to be addressed to block the sale of land if any purchased by the company or its directors.

Before framing the charge, a brief facts of the case can be provided in the final report narrating the stage by stage operations of the fraudsters which constitute the crime in the case and the documents required to prove this has to be enlisted serially.

Framing of Charge, as a compact allegations of guilt against the accused, without evading the legal content of the penal sections of law is very important for successful prosecution of the case. A model charge is provided below:

> *Charge U/S 3, 4, 5 and 6 of the Prize Chits and Money Circulations Schemes Banning Act 1978, 419, 420, 468 and 201, 204 r/w 34 IPC and Section 66 D of the Information Technology Act 2000*

That A1, named ...., a Delhi based company, with the connivance of its associate companies, i.e., Ax to Ay, had fraudulently and dishonestly conducted and promoted a pyramid model investment scheme based on binary enrollment plan, i.e., a money circulation scheme whereby the money derived from the entrance money and deposits of the new members who are subscribing to it periodically was made use of for making exorbitant payments to the previous members in the up-line, during the period from June 2012 to April 2015.

The scheme was run through a website with the domain www.abcdefg.com on the computer internet, for the making of quick and easy money, by promising fabulous return on investments in the form of various prize monies and incentives such as spot commission, loyalty commission and binary matching commission, contingent to the enrollment of new members into it, and thus Ax to Ay companies represented by A... to A... swindled and siphoned off the amounts invested by the witnesses, noted against each in the memo of evidence, totatling Rs. 100 crore from XXXXX police station limit and thereby cheated them and that the offence was committed with the consent, initiative and connivance of A... to A..., the directors, managers, and other officers of the company who were in charge of and responsible to the company for the conduct of the scheme at the time, the offence was committed and are thus guilty of the offence under sections 3, 4, 5 and 6 of the Prize Chits and Money Circulation Scheme (Banning) Act, and 420 IPC.

That, A… to A…, the senior leaders and members of the scheme, in their hot pursuit of making quick and easy money, have fraudulently and dishonestly promoted and conducted the money circulation scheme, run by A1 company, acted as agents and officers of the same, made aggressive enrollment of new members into an arithmetically infeasible scheme, by inducing the down-line members for such further enrollment which lead to viral proliferation of the network of the scheme and thereby made huge wrongful gain noted against each and wrongful loss to large number of down-line members, shown in the memo of evidence and thereby committed the offence punishable under sections 4, 5, and 6 of the Prize Chits and Money Circulation Scheme (Banning) Act and section 420 IPC.

That A… to A…, the officials and directors of the company, with the dishonest intention of camouflaging the illegal money circulation scheme under the garb of multi-level marketing or product sales, resorted to the fraudulent practice of recording the money collected from the members through subscription fee of pyramid investment scheme run by A1 company to be the sales proceeds of some products like… etc. and issued receipt, without making any actual sale or allotting any products to the members for distribution, and are thus liable to be punished for the offence of forgery for the purpose of cheating punishable under section 468 IPC.

That A… to A…, the directors and owners of AA Company, after concealing their identity by furnishing fake address in the documents produced before the registrar of Companies, had created a website with the domain www.tycoonsempire.com in the cyber space on the computer internet and had run the deceptive money circulation scheme by using this site as a means of communication, by posting offer of fabulous returns and highly glossed up success stories of team leaders, for attracting and cheating the gullible and thereby committed the offence of cheating by personating punishable under section 66 (D) of Information Technology Act and 419 IPC.

That A…. to A….the directors and officers of the companies, with the intention of tampering the evidence in this case, have delinked the data base from the website www.abcdef.com in the computer internet after making criminal conspiracy following the registration of this case and this had caused disappearance of web page containing the data base relating to down-line spreading of the network, fund flow, pay out to senior leaders, and sponsorship by each member which constitute valuable evidence in this case and thus are guilty of the offence under section 201 and 204 IPC.

Index